# Bureaucracy in
# Canadian Government

# Bureaucracy in Canadian Government

*Selected Readings*
*edited by:*

## W. D. K. Kernaghan
*Brock University*

**METHUEN**

Toronto          London          Sydney          Wellington

Library of Congress Catalog Card Number 75-89951

SBN   458   90380   9   hc

SBN   458   90390   6   pb

Printed and bound in Canada

73   72   71   70   69       2   3   4   5   6

# Preface

This book of readings is designed as an introduction to the politics and administration of the Canadian bureaucracy. The impetus for its publication comes from a desire to demonstrate to university and college students the importance of the study and practice of public administration. Failure to recognize that an examination of the administrative process is integral to understanding the Canadian political system has resulted, in part, from the simple lack of adequate reading material.

The recent publication of *Public Administration in Canada*, co-edited by the late A. M. Willms and myself, attempted to achieve broad coverage of the theoretical, managerial, and political elements of public administration. This smaller book purports to serve a more limited purpose by focusing on the intimate links between politics and administration in Canada.

The introductory part points to recent developments in the study and practice of Canadian public administration and to the prospects for change. Part Two sets within Canada's political and constitutional framework the internal management of the federal public service in the broad areas of organization, personnel, and finance. The selections in the third part concern relationships between public administrators on the one hand and politicians, pressure groups, and the general public on the other. Particular emphasis is placed on the role of public officials in the policy-making process. Finally, Part Four investigates the critical issue of the continuing expansion of the administrator's role in decision making of a legislative and judicial nature. Various existing and potential instruments of control devised to promote the administrative responsibility of public servants are also examined.

A selected bibliography is attached to each part for the direction of students wishing to read more widely on a particular topic. Although the bibliography is primarily composed of Canadian items, a list of the major textbooks in the broad field of public administration is provided at the end of Part One.

To include an appropriate number and selection of subjects in this book, substantial editing of several articles was necessary. I extend appreciation to all authors whose writings are reprinted here and particular thanks to those who permitted abridgement of their work. Any resulting deficiencies in the style or content of the contributions are the responsibility of the editor.

W.D.K.K.

# Contents

# PART THREE
## Politics and Administration

# PART FOUR
## Administrative Responsibility

# PART ONE

# Introduction to Canadian
# Public Administration

During the past twenty-five years, research on Canadian government and politics has been primarily concerned with political parties, voting behavior, and, particularly since 1960, with the financial, linguistic, and cultural aspects of Canadian federalism. Public administration, which had long enjoyed a prominent position in the study of Canadian politics, suffered a relative decline of academic interest during this period. Scholars tended to relegate the examination of administrative problems to the status of "research of last resort". In recent years, however, the increasingly apparent dominance of the bureaucracy on the output side of the political process and its near monopoly of the function of rule application has reawakened concern among academics and practitioners for the study of public administration.

The first selection in this part provides an overview of the enormous growth in numbers and influence of Canadian public servants as well as an evaluation of the status and future prospects of the study and teaching of public administration in Canada. In the second article, Canada's federal Public Service Commissioner assesses the expanding range of the public servants' functions in both new and changing areas of government activity.

# 1 Public Administration in Canada*

## W. D. Kenneth Kernaghan

## *The Growth of the Bureaucracy*

Improved management of the public's business at all levels of government in Canada is a prime determinant of this nation's capacity to realize its political, social and economic goals. Skilful and highly motivated public personnel are crucial to achieving these objectives. To minimize the influence of public servants on policy making, on the provision of a striking variety of public services and on the enforcement of regulations is to close one's eyes before overwhelming evidence.

The lingering popular image of the bureaucracy as a passive instrument of political masters serves as a convenient fiction for the politician who desires recognition as an effective policy maker and the administrator who covets his anonymity. Yet students and practitioners of public administration have long acknowledged the participation of administrators in the policy-making process and the difficulty of maintaining any well-defined structural differentiation between policy making and policy implementation. In regard to the pervasive nature of policy making, R. G. Robertson, Clerk of the Privy Council and Secretary to the Cabinet, wrote that "any civil servant above clerical or stenographic grades who has spent any substantial time in a job without contributing to some de-

---

* W. D. K. Kernaghan, "An Overview of Public Administration in Canada Today," *Canadian Public Administration*, Vol. 11, No. 3 (Fall, 1968), pp. 291-308 (reprinted and abridged by permission of author and publisher).

gree to the policy he administers should be fired".[1] Furthermore, he asserted, "the distinction is not between those who contribute to the 'making' of policy and those who do not – but between those who finally decide and those who try to carry the decided policy out, whether it is the policy they contributed to making, a caricature of it, or the very opposite".[2]

Senator Maurice Lamontagne, however, has made the provocative suggestion that the "twilight of the civil servants" is at hand. He has argued that the new centres of influence on policy making will be the intellectual community through "the rising number of Royal Commissions, task forces, advisory boards and councils"; the general public through its measured response to polls and motivation surveys; backbenchers through their increasing contributions in party caucus and in parliamentary committees; and the mass media through their control of communication.[3] This novel hypothesis remains to be proved but it points to a fruitful area for inquiry into the determinants of any given public policy. Even if the validity of the hypothesis is granted, however, effective influence may still remain with the administrators who will have less to say about *what should be done* but will continue to determine *how it should be done*.

The continuous expansion of government activities has also markedly altered the administrative process. New and challenging areas of concern have supplemented the increasingly complex task of fulfilling the traditional responsibilities for the conduct of external relations and national defence and for the administration of justice. The irreversible momentum of welfare state legislation has raised health, welfare and educational services to unprecedented heights and has greatly extended the regulation of individual and group conduct in diverse areas of socio-economic life. Canadians are intimately and continuously affected by government policy on such fundamental matters as education, federal and provincial schemes for medical care, air and water pollution, and housing. The unavoidable interdependence of all levels of government in planning programs and allocating tax revenues to discharge these obligations raises intricate problems of political accommodation and administrative coordination. Priorities among competing public demands must be established and justified. Yet setting priorities is complicated further by regional disparities in needs. Some areas of the country enjoy ample housing but suffer severely from inadequate transportation or educational facilities. Increasingly

---

[1] R. G. Robertson, "The Canadian Parliament and Cabinet in the Face of Modern Demands," *Canadian Public Administration*, Vol. 11, No. 3 (Fall, 1968), p. 272.

[2] *Ibid.*

[3] Maurice Lamontagne, "The Influence of the Politician," *Canadian Public Administration*, Vol. 11, No. 3 (Fall, 1968), p. 266.

large staffs of administrative and technical personnel are being recruited
and trained to implement government programs to meet these needs.
Indeed, approximately one out of every six members of the Canadian
labour force is now engaged in public employment.

## Recent Developments

The satisfaction of public needs and the implementation of legislation
depend on the capacity of the public services to operate in the most economical and efficient manner compatible with limitations and controls
imposed by politicians, judges, the mass media and the public. Improvement in the public services rests largely on a spirited and continuing dialogue between civil servants and outside experts and upon a reciprocal exchange of advances in the art and the science of administration. In recent
years, there has been accelerated interest, even excitement, among students and practitioners of public administration in Canada. Internal developments in the federal service in particular have aroused public consci-
ousness of the growing dynamism of both the study and the practice of
public administration. The single most powerful stimulus to popular
awareness of the need for administrative reform was the appointment
in 1960 of the Royal Commission on Government Organization (the
Glassco Commission) and the controversial proposals of the five-volume
*Report* of the Commission released between September 1962 and February 1963.[4] The Commission's terms of reference called for the recommendation of changes in the management of government departments
and agencies which "would best promote efficiency, economy and improved service in the despatch of public business". The recommendations
of the *Report* were screened by the Bureau of Government Organization
and approved by the Cabinet before the implementation of most of the
central reforms began.

Additional administrative developments have stimulated national interest in the federal public service. The Liberal Government has enacted
legislation "to encourage bilingualism in the federal public service, as
part of its fundamental objective of promoting and strengthening national
unity on the basis of the equality of rights and opportunities for both
English and French-speaking Canadians".[5] Then, in July 1967, following the 1960 *Report of the Preparatory Committee on Collective Bargaining in the Public Service*, the Public Service Staff Relations Act[6]
established a system of collective bargaining and arbitration for a large

---

4 See Donald C. Rowat, "Canada's Royal Commission on Government Organization," *Public Administration* (U.K.), Vol. 41 (Summer, 1963), pp. 193-205.
5 *Debates* (Commons) (April 6, 1966), p. 3,915.
6 *Statutes of Canada* (1966-1967), 14-15-16, Eliz. II, c. 72.

proportion of Canada's public employees. Although it is premature to attempt any meaningful evaluation of these developments in bilingualism and collective bargaining, the central importance of these reforms for the future evolution of the public service cannot be denied. The debate over these progressive measures, coupled with noteworthy studies of municipal, regional and provincial governmental administration[7] has directed widespread attention to the potential benefits of inquiries into the management of the public services. In addition, revolutionary innovations in the United States civil service, particularly the service-wide application of the Planning-Programming-Budgeting System (PPBS) which originated in the Department of Defence, have encouraged extensive study and revision of the planning and budgetary process in Canada's federal public service.[8]

## The Study and Teaching of Public Administration[9]

Despite these indications of growth and change in the Canadian public services, Canadian public administration as a field of study has not yet come of age.[10] In view of the advanced stage of the discipline in the United States, and to a lesser degree in Great Britain, the paucity of literature on Canadian public administration is staggering.[11] In the United States, academic emphasis has turned from the structural and procedural features of public administration to the sociological and psychological aspects of the bureaucracy, whereas Canadian scholars have not yet adequately explored the first stage.

---

[7] See, for example, Manitoba: Report of the Royal Commission on Local Government Organization and Finance, 1964; New Brunswick: Report of the Royal Commission on Finance and Municipal Taxation, 1963; Ontario: Report of the Royal Commission on Metropolitan Toronto, 1965; Ontario: Report of the Commission on Niagara Region Local Government Review 1966; and Saskatchewan: Report of the Royal Commission on Government Administration, 1965.

[8] See the Symposium on PPBS in *Public Administration Review*, Vol. 26 (December, 1966), pp. 243-310. See also a succinct summary of Canadian developments in this area in *Debates* (Commons) (October 10, 1967), pp. 2,933-36.

[9] See Donald C. Rowat, "The Study of Public Administration in Canada," *Public Administration* (U.K.), Vol. 40 (Autumn, 1962), pp. 319-24.

[10] For the purpose of this paper, the author accepts the very broad interpretation of "study" as embracing not only research contributions in the way of systematic analysis but also historical or contemporary accounts of administrative problems and processes.

[11] An excellent bibliography of book-length and periodical literature in public administration at all levels of Canadian government is contained in the *Selected Lists of Current Materials on Canadian Public Administration* published between 1954 and 1965 by the Carleton University Library. Note also the lists of relevant new books and articles included in issues of the journal, *Canadian Public Administration*.

The Institute of Public Administration of Canada was founded in 1949. The publication of papers delivered at its annual conferences from then until the establishment in 1958 of the quarterly journal, *Canadian Public Administration*, served as the take-off point for more vigorous examination of selected aspects of public administration in Canada. In the absence of a general textbook on Canadian public administration, students and teachers have been forced to read British and American works. The influence of American perspectives on public administration has been the more potent, however, and the content of Canadian instruction in public administration has tended to reflect American teaching. The descriptive and rather specialized Canadian works of R. M. Dawson[12] and of Taylor Cole[13] are dated now. Fortunately, in 1960 J. E. Hodgetts and D. C. Corbett compiled a useful collection of readings on Canadian public administration,[14] which focuses on organization theory, administrative practice, personnel administration, and administrative powers and responsibilities. Then, in 1968, A. M. Willms and W. D. K. Kernaghan co-edited a book of Canadian readings designed "to provide a representative selection of concepts, issues, and developments in modern public administration".[15]

Further research is essential to encourage Canadian university students to study public administration and to stimulate enthusiasm for a career in the public service. As a consequence of competition with many other fields, few Canadian departments of political science devote their resources primarily to teaching and studying public administration. Thirty of 44 universities recently surveyed[16] offered at least one undergraduate course in public administration and 11 of these provided graduate courses. In every case, the courses formed part of the program of departments of political science or political economy. Students are much less likely to be exposed to courses in provincial, local, regional or metropolitan government or any combination of these subjects at Canadian universities. The survey showed that only 16 of the 44 universities offered undergraduate courses and only five made graduate work available in one or more of these subjects.

---

[12] R. MacGregor Dawson, *The Civil Service of Canada* (Toronto, Oxford University Press, 1929).

[13] R. Taylor Cole, *The Canadian Bureaucracy* (Durham, North Carolina, Duke University Press, 1949).

[14] J. E. Hodgetts and D. C. Corbett, *Canadian Public Administration* (Toronto, The Macmillan Company of Canada Limited, 1960).

[15] A. M. Willms and W. D. K. Kernaghan, *Public Administration in Canada* (Toronto, Methuen Publications, 1968), p. ix.

[16] This survey was based on an examination of courses listed in the calendars of all the major universities in Canada.

Norton Long contends that "public administration is inevitably and deeply involved in the articulation of needs, the statement of problems, and the formulation of policy alternatives. In these tasks it is concerned with equipping its practitioners to govern wisely."[17] The Canadian federal public service cannot guarantee the wisdom of its practitioners, but it does ensure that public servants have the opportunity to receive training in the concepts and techniques of administration. The Public Service Commission of Canada, assisted by individual departments and agencies, offers extensive training and development programs not only to public servants in the Ottawa area but also to officials from federal field offices across the country. The general public should be reassured by the variety of in-service training and development programs for Canada's public servants. The composition of many of these programs is continually recast to provide public employees with the conceptual and technological skills necessary to cope with the rapidly changing nature of the administrative process.

## Prospects of Public Administration in Canada

That the study and teaching of public administration in Canada is beginning to flourish is cause for guarded optimism about accomplishments during the next decade. The status and the potential development of the subject may be assessed by classifying it into political, managerial, and socio-psychological categories. The treatment of public administration as part of the political process stimulates the political scientist to investigate such questions as the policy-making activities and ethical standards of public servants, legislative controls over the public service, and the adjustment of demands for efficiency to demands for a public service representative of ethnic, linguistic, and other special interests.[18]

Scholars and public officials disposed to examining the more practical operations of government are continuing to make significant contributions in such areas as personnel and financial management, material

---

17 Norton E. Long, "Politicians for Hire—The Dilemma of Education and the Task of Research," *Public Administration Review*, Vol. 25, No. 2 (June, 1965), p. 120.

18 Donald V. Smiley has referred to the notable studies of "public policy devices and processes" since 1945 as "those of J. E. Hodgetts on public corporations and royal commissions, of Norman Ward on parliamentary control of public expenditures, of D. C. Rowat on the Ombudsman, and of Donald Smiley on federal grants-in-aid to the provinces". See his "Contributions to Canadian Political Science since the Second World War", *Canadian Journal of Economics and Political Science*, Vol. 33, No. 4 (November, 1967), pp. 569-80.

management, and other managerial techniques. There is a special need for mathematicians and statisticians to assist in much of this practically-oriented research, particularly to promote innovations in the rapidly evolving managerial techniques of operations research and electronic data processing. The Treasury Board has already begun to meet this need through the recent creation of a new division within the Management Improvement Branch named SIMPAC (System of Integrated Management Planning and Control). The former President of the Treasury Board, E. J. Benson, has explained that

> the SIMPAC division has been staffed with highly trained specialists in such management disciplines as computer technology, operations research, economics, accounting, and program budgeting.[19]

The socio-psychological aspects of the study of public administration involve a wide range of subjects including factors affecting decision-making, styles of leadership, and the effects on individual and group behaviour of interaction between the formal and informal elements of organization. Sociologists and psychologists could assist political scientists in these areas. Equipped with sophisticated quantitative and methodological tools, they could examine traditional views on the nature of the administrative process in Canada and test hypotheses with more precise techniques of measurement.

Informed scholars and practitioners are conscious of the rapidly expanding and nebulous boundaries of the study of administration. The emphasis on the behavioural approach to the subject and its growing links with other social sciences have given an inter-disciplinary bent to inquiries into administrative systems. The inter-disciplinary nature of administrative inquiry does not require the separation of public administration from political science as some scholars have suggested. It does, however, demand that instructors keep themselves informed of developments in other disciplines affecting the teaching and the practice of public administration. Furthermore, it is essential that social scientists collaborate in their research efforts and incorporate the contributions of scholars in other disciplines.

---

[19] *Debates* (Commons) (October 10, 1967), p. 2,935.

# 2 The Changing Scope of the Canadian Public Servant*

## J. J. Carson

The rapid social, economic, and technical changes in our society have touched all of us, from the "hippie" who opts out, to the manager who wonders if he will become obsolete in the advancing age of automation. There is little doubt that our society is changing at a pace never before witnessed; concepts, techniques, and environments – all are changing. We are likely to have a greater number and a greater variety of problems in the next ten years than we have had in the last one hundred. As public administrators we must be able to respond to these changes, and that response will not always be easy.

There are at least six major changes that will directly alter the scope of public administration in Canada: automation, biculturalism, the growth of the welfare state, international service, collective bargaining, and the managerial philosophy of J. Grant Glassco. These have not been listed in order of importance because they will vary in their significance for each public servant. But sooner or later they will affect nearly all public servants whether they are employed at the federal, the provincial or the municipal level of government. The image of the whole public service depends on the resiliency and the imagination of all its members. Their capacity to respond to change at all levels may well help to determine the future of this country.

* J. J. Carson, "The Changing Scope of the Public Servant," *Canadian Public Administration,* Vol. 11, No. 4 (Winter, 1968), pp. 407-13 (reprinted and slightly abridged by permission of author and publisher).

# I. Automation

The first force for change is automation, or more properly, cybernation – the science of communication and control. This particular advance alone will give us the ability to organize technical and social processes rationally on a scale never before possible. In the years since the industrial revolution, knowledge of the techniques of production has led to widespread industrialization. This has been an extremely rapid development if one considers how long man lived in the agricultural age. But for all its rapidity, this growth will be seen as a relatively slow process in comparison with the changes taking place today.

All of us are dimly aware of the potential uses of the computer in public administration, and much experimental activity in this sphere is now under way. Public services generally, however, are still lagging behind their industrial counterparts in embracing the full potential and implications of the cybernetic age. Computers are not only capable of giving us better mechanization in our present organizations. They can give us the potential for something entirely different. Computers can enable us to analyze the whole of our operations in a detail and scope never before possible. In fact, computers are misused if they are merely a means of speeding up present calculating processes. They should be used for insight, not reckoning. Such use will demand an ability and perceptiveness that many a maintenance-oriented manager lacks. Information provided by automation will be a key resource, and, in the future, governments are likely to have a near monopoly of it.

For this reason it is essential that the public administrator of tomorrow have understanding and conviction about the potentialities of these new tools and that he embrace them with confidence. Automation can drastically change the scope of the public servant's activities and contributions – but only if he is prepared for change.

# II. Biculturalism

At the federal level of government, we are deeply committed to the establishment of a bilingual and bicultural public service. Only in this way can we ensure that public policy and its administration will adequately reflect the values and sentiments of the two founding races. This is no easy task and for middle-aged public servants it is a slow and painful process. Fortunately, for our young university graduates it is proving to be much easier.

Regardless of the difficulty, we are determined to have a bilingual and, hopefully, bicultural administration within ten years. This will indeed change the scope of the federal public servant's occupation. For those who work with the provinces and the municipalities, there is an important challenge in this development that should not be ignored or brushed aside. In our federal language schools, a person starting from total ignorance can speak a second language quite fluently after 1200 hours of instruction. On the basis of 200 teaching days a year and one hour a day, a student could become bilingual in six years. Surely this is an attainable objective in the Canadian public school systems.

As long as Canadians can barely read their second official language, let alone speak it, there can be little real communication among us, and our present difficulties will not be resolved. When English and French-speaking Canadians can talk to one another in their mother tongues and, at last, understand one another, we shall have taken an enormous step forward in preserving this bicultural country of ours. The responsibility for this advance rests with the provinces and the municipalities. For those in the federal public service, there is the new and challenging opportunity to work in a truly bicultural milieu.

## III. The Growth of the Welfare State

This rather hackneyed phrase is used to describe the continual growth and proliferation of government activity in all facets of our society. The demand for increased services from all levels of government seems relentless and insatiable. We must accept the fact that, regardless of a government's political persuasion, it will inevitably find itself providing more and, hopefully, better services to its citizens than did its predecessors.

This will mean a continually expanding public service with more and more interesting and potentially rewarding jobs to be performed – "potentially rewarding" because so much depends on our being able to organize these tasks in a way that makes them meaningful and challenging to the public servants. If we merely expand our bureaucratic army of clerical workers whenever a new program is launched, we shall have done little to satisfy the demands of the citizenry and even less to make the public service a vital and demanding career. Too often we embark on socially useful programs with inadequately trained staff. The result is a paper-pushing, highly regulated exercise that often seems devoid of human understanding or imagination. The necessity to entrust the administration of funds – on some occasions – to individuals lacking professional qualifications forces us to hedge them in with controls and rule books. Nothing is more deadening or emasculating to a dedicated public servant than to discover that in certain circumstances "the law is an ass" but that he must defend it.

It appears that we are now breaking out of these traditional patterns. Risk-taking is more and more recognized as the only valid approach to some of today's complicated social problems, particularly in the field of corrections and some of our related community disorders. The growth of the welfare state is going to bring new and grave challenges to the public servant. If we are to deal with these problems effectively, we must assume new attitudes and approaches to public administration. We must become more courageous, more imaginative, and more virile.

## IV. *International Service*

The increasing opportunities for Canadian citizens to work abroad represent another aspect of the changing scope of the public service. For years, Canada has had a distinguished but relatively small foreign service. It has been composed of a rather elite group of public servants who have brought great distinction to the nation and honour to themselves. A foreign service officer appointment still ranks as a prized goal amongst the ablest young people in the country, as evidenced by the number and quality of university graduates who enter our annual foreign service competitions.

It is notable that the diplomatic monopoly on international service is becoming a thing of the past. This year there are thousands of young and not-so-young Canadians serving abroad with External Aid, Canadian University Students Overseas, the Ford Foundation, our own Immigration Branch, and the various agencies of the United Nations. They are sharing the skills and experiences of Canada with the developing nations of Asia and Africa, particularly in the field of public administration. These efforts are building a solid reputation for the competency, the integrity, and the goodwill of Canadians. Perhaps the most important element of the activities of Canadian public servants working overseas is that their own horizons are broadened. As Canada expands its aid programs and its support of international agencies, there will be increasing opportunities for public administrators from all levels of government to volunteer their skills and know-how in the sphere of international service.

## V. *Collective Bargaining*

In March, 1967, the federal Parliament enacted legislation that formally introduced collective bargaining as a legal method for regulating relationships between the State as employer and public servants as employees. In some respects, the federal government was merely following the municipalities and certain provinces in taking this step. In other respects, it was pioneering, particularly with regard to its decision to design a special piece of legislation tailored to the special needs of the public service, one that sets the stage for a more mature and civilized relationship than generally exists across the country. Only time can tell whether all these high hopes will be realized.

There is already, however, abundant evidence within the federal service that the new collective bargaining regime is paving the way for a more wholesome approach to the whole business of staff relations. The old, rather sentimental, sometimes sloppy, sometimes indifferent, "noblesse oblige" approach is quickly disappearing. Public administrators are waking up to the fact that they have a responsibility for staff relations and that their administration must be fair, sensible, and consistent. The individual supervisor can no longer shift blame to some mysterious "they" – presumably the old Civil Service Commission or the Treasury Board. Now, the supervisor must stand on his own feet, assume responsibility for his actions or decisions, and then be prepared to have them challenged through the grievance procedure all the way up to independent and binding adjudication. This can be a very cathartic experience. Inevitably, there will be some growing pains during the first few years as old-time administrators will resent and misinterpret the comparative weakness of their position in staff relationships, and some over-zealous staff association officials will take advantage of these changed conditions for short term gains. Gradually, these trial and error struggles will settle down into a healthy, mutually self-respecting relationship between the public administrator and organized labour. The achievement of collective bargaining is an irreversible change in the federal service and I believe that it is an inevitable one in the provincial services.

## VI. The Ghost of Glassco

Finally, there is the potential for change resulting from the managerial philosophy set forth by J. Grant Glassco in the Report of the Royal Commission on Government Organization. In effect, Glassco not only said "let the managers manage" but "require them to manage". Regardless of how much one may want to quarrel with Glassco on detail, there is no question that his philosophy of management responsibility is going to have an enduring effect on the future of public administration in Canada. It took almost two decades for the Brownlow Report (Report of the President's Committee on Administrative Management – 1937) to influence public administration in the United States but eventually the political science students who read Brownlow in their college days became the senior administrators of government. And change came about! Moreover, a new generation of public administrators have read the Glassco Report, and by and large they like what they have read. It is encouraging also that Glassco's philosophy does not belong to one man, to one Royal Commission or to one political party. The philosophy of management is well supported by all the theorists and practitioners who have ever seriously studied the problems of administration in large-scale, dispersed organizations.

Let us, therefore, embrace this philosophy of management responsibility in the public service. Let us genuinely show that we are capable of acting responsibly, that we are willing to be held accountable, that we do care about the taxpayers' dollars – in a word – that we can manage. Too long the public administrator has been caricatured as an empire-building bureaucrat who, if given a chance, will fulfill all of Professor Parkinson's worst fears. We are doing everything we can to eradicate this image at the federal level of government. I believe that we are having some success as recent recruiting efforts at the universities across the country have brought an enormous increase in the number of persons recruited, without loss of quality.

But recruiting figures and external image-building are not a complete answer to the problems and challenges of the public service. We must set about to create a really lively, invigorating atmosphere within the public service – and at all levels of government. I am just as concerned with creating a climate that will encourage stenographers to tell their bosses that stenography is an inefficient and obsolete art as I am with encouraging managers to face up to the fact that automation may relieve them of half their staff but enable them to be twice as effective. This is the kind of environment that the public service must generate.

# Part One

*READINGS*

*General*

Dimock, M. E. and Dimock, G. M., *Public Administration*. 4th ed. New York, Holt, Rinehart and Winston, Inc., 1969.

Gladden, E. N., *An Introduction to Public Administration*. London, Staples Press Limited, 1966.

Gladden, E. N., *Essentials of Public Administration*. London, Staples Press Limited, 1964.

Golembiewski, R. T., et al., eds., *Public Administration: Readings in Institutions, Processes and Behavior*. Chicago, Rand McNally & Company, 1966.

Hawley, C. E. and Weintraub, R. G., *Administrative Questions and Political Answers*. Princeton, N.J., D. Van Nostrand, 1966.

Hilling, Helen C., "Public Administration: Study, Practice, Profession." *Public Administration Review*, Vol. 26, No. 4 (December, 1966), pp. 320-28.

Morstein Marx, F., ed., *Elements of Public Administration*. Englewood Cliffs, N.J., Prentice-Hall, Inc., 1965.

Nigro, Felix A., *Modern Public Administration*. New York, Harper and Row, Publishers, 1965.

Pfiffner, J. M. and Presthus, R. V., *Public Administration*, 5th ed. New York, The Ronald Press Company, 1967.

Rowat, Donald C., ed., *Basic Issues in Public Administration*. New York, The Macmillan Company, 1961.

Simon, Herbert A., Smithburg, D. W., and Thompson, V. A., *Public Administration*. New York, Alfred A. Knopf, 1950.

Waldo, Dwight, *The Study of Public Administration*. New York, Random House, Inc., 1955.

Waldo, Dwight, "Public Administration." *The Journal of Politics*, Vol. 30, No. 2 (May, 1968), pp. 443-79.

White, L. D., *Introduction to the Study of Public Administration*. New York, The Macmillan Company, 1955.

*Canadian*

Brownstone, Meyer, "The Canadian System of Government in the Face of Modern Demands." *Canadian Public Administration*, Vol. 11, No. 4 (Winter, 1968), pp. 428-39.

Cole, Taylor, *The Canadian Bureaucracy, 1939-1947*. Durham, N.C., Duke University Press, 1949.

Deutsch, J. J., "The Public Service in a Changing Society." *Canadian Public Administration*, Vol. 11, No. 1 (Spring, 1968), pp. 1-8.

Downey, Lawrence W., "Administration as a Field of Inquiry." *Canadian Public Administration*, Vol. 5, No. 3 (September, 1962), pp. 359-66.

Hodgetts, J. E., "Challenge and Response: A Retrospective View of the Public Service." *Canadian Public Administration*, Vol. 7, No. 4 (December, 1964), pp. 409-21.

Hodgetts, J. E. and Corbett, D. C., eds., *Canadian Public Administration: A Book of Readings*. Toronto, The Macmillan Company of Canada, Limited, 1960.

Hodgetts, J. E., *Pioneer Public Service: An Administrative History of the United Canadas, 1841-1867*. Toronto, University of Toronto Press, 1955.

Johanson, H., "Towards an Aggregate Analysis of Public Service." *Canadian Public Administration*, Vol. 9, No. 3 (September, 1966), pp. 367-75.

Kernaghan, W. D. K., "An Overview of Public Administration in Canada Today." *Canadian Public Administration*, Vol. 11, No. 3( Fall, 1968), pp. 291-308.

Porter, John, *The Vertical Mosaic: An Analysis of Social Class and Power in Canada.* Toronto, University of Toronto Press, 1965, Chap. 14.

Rowat, Donald C., "The Study of Public Administration in Canada." *Public Administration*, (U.K.), Vol. 40 (Autumn, 1962), pp. 319-24.

Willms, A. M. and Kernaghan, W. D. K., eds., *Public Administration in Canada: Selected Readings.* Toronto, Methuen Publications, 1968.

# PART TWO

# Organization, Personnel, and Finance

Revolutionary changes in the internal management of the federal public service have occurred and are continuing to occur from implementation of the recommendations of the Royal Commission on Government Organization. The Commission's Report (The Glassco Report), published in 1962 and 1963, brought about particularly notable changes in the inter-related areas of organization, personnel management, and financial management. In this part, the current state of internal management in these three areas of central concern is described. Important administrative issues arising from Canada's federal system are also examined.

The first two articles by A. M. Willms explore the structural relations between the Cabinet and government departments, the typical organization of a department, and the functions and diversity of crown agencies. Then, Taylor Cole and Edgar Gallant discuss federal-provincial administrative machinery for intergovernmental liaison, and Sylvain Cloutier assesses measures promoting bilingualism and biculturalism among senior public servants. R. H. Dowdell sets personnel management in its political environment and touches on such significant personnel matters as merit systems, career planning, and training. Finally, H. R. Balls provides a succinct but comprehensive summary of financial administration in Canada, including an explanation of the budgetary process.

# 3 The Executive and the Departmental Structure*

## A. M. Willms

## *The Executive*

Cabinet ministers in Canada bear extremely heavy responsibilities both as members of Parliament and as the top executives of government departments. Although the legislative and executive roles of ministers overlap, attention will be focussed here on their executive functions as members of the Cabinet and heads of administrative departments.

The executive tasks of ministers have been well stated by the Glassco Commission:

> . . . ministers need not be administrative experts; on the contrary, it is desirable save in the stress of emergencies, that they do not become deeply involved in the administrative process. As members of the Cabinet, their principal obligation is to reflect and give effect to the collective point of view – drawing together the public interests, attitudes and aspirations that find expression in the political process, and, by reconciling these, providing the basis for an essential unity of government in policy and action. As heads of departments, it is the task of ministers to define the ends to be pursued, and to instill their own sense of purpose and of urgency in the permanent officials.[1]

* A. M. Willms, *Organization in Canadian Government Administration*. Unpublished manual (revised and abridged by the editor), Carleton University, Ottawa, 1965.

[1] *Royal Commission on Government Organization,* Vol. 5 (Ottawa, Queen's Printer, 1963), p. 33.

For each government department there is a Cabinet minister who takes full responsibility for its actions and who is credited with its achievements. Each minister is responsible to Parliament for the operation of his department and by convention the act of every public servant in the department is regarded as the act of the minister. The extent to which a minister can in fact be held accountable for the maladministration of his departmental subordinates is not clear. In practice, a minister's survival under such circumstances depends largely on his influence within his party and whether the party feels it can face criticism of its administration without being defeated in Parliament or at the next election.

The Canadian Cabinet tends to be excessively large in membership because the Prime Minister traditionally appoints ministers to meet the demands for representation of provinces and regions and of ethnic, linguistic, and religious groups. Clearly, the Prime Minister must take account of such a crucial political consideration despite possible adverse effects on the fulfillment of administrative needs. Canada now has twenty-five federal departments and about four times as many agencies. The number and diversity of these administrative units creates a span of control that is far too wide for a Cabinet which has onerous political and constitutional responsibilities. The Glassco Commission, however, recognized the primacy of political factors over administrative interests in organizing the executive structure of government:

> Above all, the organization of government, no less than the policies it pursues, must reflect the order of importance, in the minds of the public, of the problems requiring attention. Unless there is, in rough form, this correlation between the content of ministerial posts and the degree of public concern, government policy and action will almost certainly fail to respond adequately to public wants.[2]

Indeed, new departments or agencies may have to be established to emphasize or point up a new government policy. It may not be sufficient merely to enunciate new functions and allot these to an existing department or agency. To give these government activities prominence in the public mind another administrative unit may have to be created. The establishment of Central Mortgage and Housing Corporation immediately after the war and of the Department of Consumer and Corporate Affairs in 1967 are striking examples of this need. Since it is very difficult to dissolve a governmental unit once it has been set up, the number of units tends to increase.

A good case can be made on administrative-managerial grounds for fewer, more uniform, and necessarily larger administrative units. The following comments pertain specifically to departments although they are

---

2 *Ibid.,* pp. 41-42.

generally applicable to government agencies also. The overhead cost for adequate departmental services in small units may be disproportionately large, and the provision of such services as organization and methods or research and development may not be warranted. In addition, the existence of larger departments permits much more coherent government planning. Central control agencies such as the Treasury Board and the Public Service Commission can more readily stay out of planning when the allocation of scarce resources can be thrashed out in a few large departments. For example, if all the labour functions, including unemployment insurance, were centred in one department, the Treasury Board would be less concerned with the proportion of funds that should go to each of the various governmental units in the labour field. Larger departments also provide a wider field of training, development and advancement for capable junior and intermediate staff. The advantages of specialization can best be realized in larger departments, whether in the line functions, the staff functions, or the departmental services. A substantial measure of decentralization is almost inevitable in larger departments and with fewer, but more comprehensive, field offices, the government can expect greater effectiveness with smaller overhead costs. Moreover, in a federal state many government activities require consultation and coordination between provincial and federal administrators; fewer and larger departments would make such cooperation easier.

There are, however, persuasive arguments for a large number of smaller departments. Individual ministers and deputy ministers can handle a small department more effectively than a large department. This is not so much a factor of size in manpower or budget as of political sensitivity and diversity of functions. The more sensitive the departmental functions in the political-social-economic atmosphere of the day, the more care must be given to policy decisions and the more skill must be employed in representing the department to the Cabinet, Parliament and the public. The more diverse the functions, the more overall policies must be coordinated by the man who must answer to Parliament for their implementation.

Instead of decreasing the size of any department, perhaps the functions of government could be redistributed so that similar functions would come under one responsibility and the diversity of some of the larger departments would be decreased. Such a reallocation could actually reduce the number of departments.

## Departmental Structure

In general, the structure of departments resembles the normal scalar pyramid of private or corporate enterprise. At the top is the deputy minister who is the administrative head of the department and at the bottom are the numerous employees who actually carry out most of the functions of the department. In between are the various levels of supervision, management and specialization which make up the pyramidal structure. There is some uniformity in the terminology used to describe departmental organization at or near the pyramid's peak. The deputy minister or deputy head is at the pinnacle; below him there are assistant deputy ministers, or in a few instances, associate deputy ministers. Below the assistant deputy minister in the departmental pyramid are the branch heads who are usually called Directors or Directors-General. The branches are often further subdivided into divisions with Directors or Chiefs in charge. The divisions are subdivided in turn into what may be called sections, units, groups, services, staff, offices, or detachments and the head of each may carry any one of a great variety of titles.

The deputy minister often has a staff to assist him in his management of the department and he may also retain direct control of one or several of the branches or of the administrative services. Sometimes the deputy minister has a government agency reporting to him. Thus the Deputy Minister of Agriculture has the Director of Prairie Farm Rehabilitation and the Board of Grain Commissioners reporting to him. The span of control of a deputy minister may cover anywhere from two or three to twelve or more subordinates. Most departments have only two or three assistant deputy ministers but as the size of departments increases this number will grow.

The planning and organization of an individual department's internal structure requires a different approach from that which is taken in dividing up the functions of government between departments and agencies. The different approaches reflect the different objectives involved. In the division of the total functions of government among administrative units, the primary aim is to allot functions to a structure that satisfies political and public needs. Although the aim of the internal organization of a department or agency is to carry out the assigned functions as efficiently and effectively as possible, the minister's political and constitutional role remains an important determinant of the final structure. An organization plan should

(a) recognize the division of powers between the federal and provincial governments; in sensitive areas of jurisdiction even the appearance of federal overlapping into provincial fields must be avoided unless government policy on the subject is clear;

(b) recognize that the government exists to serve the people; recommendations that are administratively sound must also be acceptable to the segment of the population the agency has been set up to serve. In field organizations, in particular, it is sometimes necessary to modify organization principles to meet such a situation and to provide for local requirements;

(c) recognize that the minister concerned is one member of the Cabinet and that the functions of the agency, including the funds necessary for carrying them out, are often subject to balancing mechanisms within the Cabinet which supersede purely administrative considerations. Recommendations which propose the extension of an agency's functions into areas where other agencies have an interest, for instance, should be made only after the most careful exploration with the agencies concerned.[3]

In planning the department's structure, an initial decision must be made as to whether the parts of the department will be organized according to the criteria of purpose, process, clientele, or area. In the past, the factor of purpose (or function) has probably been given too much prominence in the building of branches, divisions and sections of departments. It is unwise to assume that if purpose is used to allocate the job to the department that it can also be used consistently in designing the whole departmental structure. It is often quite undesirable to emphasize the purpose factor within the department because

(a) design of departmental branches or divisions by purpose often results in too much emphasis in each branch or division on a small part of the department's overall functions; there may be too much concern for the parts and not enough for the final product;

(b) subdivision by purpose leaves little scope for competition between units which is an effective form of setting work standards and motivating units and employees;

(c) specialization by purpose can lead to overspecialization with attendant difficulties in effective employee development.

There probably isn't a department or an agency that does not use all four organization factors in one way or another. It is the manager's responsibility to choose the factor or factors applicable and to decide to what extent each is necessary. In this decision consistency appears to have little virtue and the manager may combine the use of several or all of the factors as circumstances dictate.

---

[3] Civil Service Commission, *The Analysis of Organization in the Government of Canada* (Ottawa, Queen's Printer, 1964), pp. 13-14.

# 4 Crown Agencies*

## A. M. Willms

In the British political tradition Cabinet ministers take complete responsibility for the actions of government departments, but a great part of government administration is carried out by non-departmental units called agencies which have varying amounts of ministerial surveillance.

Like many other governments the Canadian federal government has a wide range in the types of administrative units it uses to put its objectives and policies into practice. The Financial Administration Act of 1951, with subsequent amendments, divides these as follows:

| | |
|---|---|
| Government departments | 25 |
| Departmental corporations | 13 |
| Agency corporations | 15 |
| Proprietary corporations | 14 |
| Designated as departments for purposes of this Act | 46[1] |

The Act classifies government units for the purpose of clarifying their budgetary relations with the Treasury Board and with Parliament, and it uses both financial practices and agency functions to effect the classification. The definitions which result leave a lot of gaps and a great deal of overlapping; neither the definition nor the classification is satisfactory for

* A. M. Willms and W. D. K. Kernaghan, *Public Administration in Canada* (Toronto, Methuen Publications, 1968), pp. 159-66.

1 Financial Administration Act, R.S. 1952, C. 116 as amended to September, 1967. Schedules A, B, C and D.

purposes other than those of the Act. For instance, in the last category it leaves in one catch-all-class the commissions, royal commissions, boards, the Auditor General, the Chief Electoral Officer, the Privy Council Office, the National Library, and many others varying in structure, functions, methods and in almost every administrative feature. Nor is the list which the act presents exhaustive. It lists more than 100 units; the number varies from year to year; but this is not complete. It does not name agencies whose finances are regulated entirely by the creating statute such as the Bank of Canada, the Canadian Wheat Board or the Board of Grain Commissioners. Nor does it include those agencies which for budget purposes are closely affiliated to a government department such as the Dominion Bureau of Statistics, the Agricultural Prices Support Board or the Defence Research Board, or those agencies which have provincial as well as federal representation such as the Canadian Corporation for the 1967 World's Fair, the Eastern Rockies Forest Conservation Board and the Canadian Council of Resource Ministers.

There are a great number of types of units in the governmental administrative net with a wide range of functions, of organization and of procedures and no classification that is useful for purposes of discussion and study has been devised. But it is possible to distinguish departments from the assortment of corporations, boards, commissions and others which are generally labelled *agencies*. Some of the more obvious differences are

1. Departments are answerable directly to a Cabinet minister and that minister takes responsibility for their actions. Agencies usually have a minister designated to them through whom they report to Parliament but the degree of supervision and accountability varies and is much smaller than that with departments. When questioned in Parliament on the activities or policies of an agency the minister who reports for that agency will frequently disclaim responsibility: "this is a matter involving an independent agency and I can answer only in so far as the agency sees fit to provide me with the information".[2]

2. Departments are all subject to the estimates system of budgeting, that is, revenues coming from the Crown must be spent exactly as directed by Parliament and Treasury Board, and receipts must be returned to the Receiver-General. Agencies vary widely in their budget practices.

3. The personnel of departments are generally recruited by the Public Service Commission and their promotion and transfer is closely supervised by the Commission. There have always been exceptions: departments

---

[2] J. E. Hodgetts and D. C. Corbett, *Canadian Public Administration* (Toronto, Macmillan Company of Canada Limited, 1960), p. 199.

have recruited their own day labor – prevailing-rate employees – and those in a few other categories such as postmasters in revenue post offices, ships crews and some employees of overseas offices have been exempt from the Commission's authority. Only a few of the agencies recruit through the Public Service Commission. Generally speaking they are responsible for their own personnel matters.

4. Departments have deputy ministers as the administrative heads while agencies vary widely in the nature of their management. Some have boards of directors, others have chairmen, commissioners, or directors.

It is also commonly accepted that a short-term purpose is to be served by an agency while the long-term, continuing functions more often rate the creation of a department. Thus the numerous wartime enterprises of the government took the form of agencies while the long-term function of caring for veterans was incorporated in a department. Royal commissions are a group that is obviously set up on an *ad hoc* basis. But many agencies are set up for the long-term, such as the CNR and the CBC, and there have been departments such as Soldiers Civil Reestablishment created for a short-term function. It is also suggested that departments are set up to carry out functions that would not normally be tackled by private enterprise while agencies frequently compete with private business. This has a grain of truth but once again there are a number of exceptions; the Department of Public Works, the Department of Industry, Trade and Commerce, and other departments carry on activities commonly found in private business.

We have seen that departments can be distinguished from the agencies. The departments are a group that has some semblance of uniformity in its ranks, but this cannot be said of the agencies. They are just about as diverse as can be, but even so we can discern a few classes among them. One type of agency that has a title and has been treated as a genre is the Crown Corporation. This group is described fully in the Glassco Commission *Report*[3] and its members are readily distinguishable because they are identified in the Financial Administration Act. The Crown Corporation can be defined as an institution operating a service of an economic or social character on behalf of the government, but it possesses most of the legal and commercial attributes of private enterprise. Though largely autonomous in management it is still responsible to the public and subject to some direction by the government.[4]

---

[3] Royal Commission on Government Organization, Vol. 5 (Ottawa, Queen's Printer, 1963), pp. 58-75.
[4] W. Friedmann, *The Public Corporation* (Toronto, The Carswell Company Limited, 1954), p. 541.

Crown corporations are created in two ways – by special statute or by incorporation by order-in-council under the Companies Act. There are about a dozen of the latter and they form another distinguishable group known as Crown companies and carry the commercial designation "Limited" in their name. This little flourish is of course meaningless.

> (the corporate device) . . . provides a means by which a group of individuals, the shareholders, can band together to create a legal personality, the corporation, the existence of which is unaffected by the withdrawal or even the death of individual shareholders, and toward which the financial obligations of the shareholders are limited to the share capital they have subscribed. None of these things is of any relevance to a government organization . . . It is inconceivable that a corporation could survive the extinction of its sole shareholder, the Government of Canada. It is equally inconceivable, in terms of political realities, that the government would ever claim a limited liability and permit the organization to be forced into liquidation by its creditors.[5]

The parliamentary authority for the creation of Crown companies is found in any one of a number of acts which give ministers the power to procure the incorporation of bodies for carrying out the purposes of the act. The Defence Production Act, the Research Act and others carry this proviso.

The Financial Administration Act has divided the Crown corporations into three classes. The departmental corporation "is a servant or agent of Her Majesty in right of Canada and is responsible for administrative, supervisory or regulatory services of a governmental nature".[6] Examples of this class are the National Research Council and the Unemployment Insurance Commission. The second class of Crown corporation is the agency corporation which is defined as "an agent of Her Majesty in right of Canada and is responsible for the management of trading or service operations on a quasi-commercial basis, or for the management of procurement, construction or disposal activities . . ."[7] Typical examples are the Crown Assets Disposal Corporation, Canadian Arsenals and the National Harbours Board. Lastly, there are the proprietary corporations, "any Crown corporation that (i) is responsible for the management of lending or financial operations, or for the management of commercial and industrial operations involving the production of or the dealing in goods and the supplying of services to the public, and (ii) is ordinarily required to conduct its operations without appropriations".[8] Examples are the

---

5 Royal Commission on Government Organization, *op. cit.*, p. 69.
6 Financial Administration Act, Part VIII, para. 76.
7 *Ibid.*
8 *Ibid.*

CBC, Central Mortgage and Housing Corporation and Air Canada. The purpose of these definitions is to classify these agencies in their budgetary relations with Parliament and the government but there are also a few other distinguishing features in these groups. Thus no departmental corporations are created under the Companies Act while there are about half-a-dozen Crown companies in each of the agency and proprietary classes. No agency or proprietary corporations are subject to the Public Service Employment Act while one third of the departmental corporations are. All departmental and agency corporations are audited by the Auditor-General's staff while three proprietary corporations choose their own auditors. However, all Crown corporations are uniformly required to submit annual reports to their ministers.

Another form of government agency which can be distinguished is the royal commission. Royal commissions may be appointed by order-in-council under the authority of the Inquiries Act, and their function is usually to gather information on a specific topic which is of concern to the government.

Besides Crown corporations and royal commissions there is a whole host of other agencies ranging from the permanent quasi-judicial such as the Tax Appeal Board, to the *ad hoc* administrative, for example, the Bureau of Government Organization. There is no common pattern in the organization, staffing or procedures of these bodies.

Questions inevitably arise: Why do these agencies exist? Does this diversity in government administration serve a purpose? The agencies have been defined as "those creatures of expediency designed to meet the special needs arising out of the complexity of government",[9] but why could existing departments not serve these special needs?

Dean Thomas McLeod has suggested that the agencies have been created because of popular misconceptions concerning the public service. These include the belief that senior public servants are more docile and less sensitive than their business counterparts, that departmental administration invariably attracts routine and red tape, and that political direction is interference motivated by ignorance, stupidity, venality, nepotism and graft.[10] There can be no doubt that one of the purposes in creating such agencies as the Canadian National Railways and the Canadian Broadcasting Corporation was to keep them from detailed political control and therefore from political interference. The history of the Inter-colonial Rail-

---

[9] L. C. Audette, Q.C., Chairman, Tariff Board, in a talk to Junior Administrative Officer Class 1954.

[10] Institute of Public Administration of Canada, *Proceedings* (Toronto, University of Toronto Press, 1956), pp. 153 ff.

ways suggested to the government of Sir Robert Borden that the newly acquired government railways would be much better off with a management that would feel truly independent in the appointment of staff, the location of railway stations and other similar matters which had hitherto been subject to political patronage.[11] Today the departments are more adequately shielded than the agencies from patronage in appointments and contracts by those watchdogs the Public Service Commission, the Treasury Board and the Auditor-General, and following Sir Robert's logic the CNR should now become a department.

It is desirable to keep politically sensitive functions such as broadcasting, the redistribution of electoral seats, the investigations of commissions and quasi-judicial actions from the detailed supervision of government and such activities can profit from the political aloofness of an agency. It is much more difficult to justify the difference between departments and agencies in controls over personnel and financial management. There appears to be a general concensus that the facility of expeditious hiring, firing and promotion, the privilege of fixing salaries and allocating budgets without the double check of the Public Service Commission and Treasury Board has made agencies generally more effective than many departments and that it would be undesirable to hedge them about with the restrictions which departments have to accept. This leaves the uncomfortable question: If these detailed management controls lessen effectiveness why must departments suffer them?

Some of the agencies such as Polymer Rubber, Air Canada, Canadian National Railways, Eldorado, St. Lawrence Seaway and several others are organized to carry on activities in direct competition with private industry. Therefore, they feel that they must be free to copy commercial practices in such areas as trade secrecy, legal accessibility, and investment without detailed justification before a board of civil servants, business decisions based on business considerations rather than government policy and so on. Moreover, these agencies find that their dealings with other enterprises, such as contractors and suppliers, are easier, and staff development and training is simpler when the organization resembles that of the other enterprises with which it is in daily contact.

Our federal constitution as interpreted by the courts does not permit the federal and provincial levels of government to share each others' functions or to delegate responsibilities one to the other. With ingenuity, the consequent inflexibility can be modified. Agencies can be staffed by personnel who are "coincidentally" acceptable to both governments. This

---

11 *Debates* (Commons) (May 15, 1918), p. 1,999; see also a statement of Sir Thomas White, p. 1,634.

would be difficult to do in a department. The National Battlefields Commission, the Halifax Relief Commission, the Eastern Rockies Forest Conservation Board and various marketing boards have proved efficacious in bridging this constitutional gap.

Agencies set up in the form of boards or commissions permit the representation of a diversity of interests as with the Board of Broadcast Governors or the representation of interested groups as in the labor and management representation in the Unemployment Insurance Commission.

Lastly, the agencies provide a device which helps to make distasteful political ideas acceptable to the Canadian public. Socialism or the nationalization of activities which are normally in the field of private enterprise is unpopular in Canada. The political parties advocating socialism have, as a rule, had fairly slim backing but our governments have found it expedient to put into practice many socialist ideas and when the government takes over the operation of such functions as the manufacture and distribution of electricity or the retailing of liquor it does this with devices which have little connection in the public mind with public ownership of enterprise. The agencies are acceptable politically because they are different. They are not identified with the civil service in the public mind and therefore are considered quite proper competitors with private enterprise.

We have noted that in the conglomeration of government agencies there is this common pattern: a tendency to independence from detailed ministerial control and a freedom from the restraints of the Public Service Commission and Treasury Board. Does this mean that agencies can be independent of government policy, that they can act irresponsibly without regard to government or Parliamentary supervision? Far from it. Both Parliament and Cabinet have a number of ways in which they can control the functions and actions of these agencies. These controls have not always been exercised but they do exist.

The Cabinet appoints the directors or commissioners or board members who are the heads of the agencies. Usually it is the Cabinet collectively, the Governor-in-Council, which makes the appointments although sometimes individual ministers are charged with this responsibility. The heads may be appointed for a set period of time; three years, five years, seven years and ten years are popular periods, although "during pleasure" is used in almost one third of the statutes. Most statutes of incorporation state that heads may be reappointed and none bar further terms of office. Some heads may be "removed for cause" while in other statutes this is not explicit. The experience of the Diefenbaker government with the dismissal of James Coyne from the post of Governor of the Bank of Canada will probably lead other governments to hesitate before attempting similar measures, but it is established that the government can dismiss as well as appoint the heads of agencies.

Another measure of control is exercised by the appointment of those as heads of an agency who are already responsible to the minister in another capacity. Thus senior public servants, such as the deputy minister, the assistant deputy minister, or other senior men in a department may serve as directors or board members of an agency and in at least 20 agencies civil servants are members of the board.

> In most cases the civil servants are drawn from departments having a particular interest in the operations of the agency concerned. They constitute, in effect, an interdepartmental committee advising the chief executive of the agency concerned. . . . It is one thing for ministers to disclaim responsibility for the affairs of undertakings having a board of management with independent status; but it would seem to be quite a different matter when the board consists of or is controlled by permanent officials, each of whom is answerable to his own minister for his actions.[12]

Some provinces have gone one step further in that they have appointed ministers to the directorates of agencies. This practice seems to have been forestalled in the federal government by the declaration of the father of many agencies, Hon. C. D. Howe, that "the board will function very much better if no minister of the Crown is a member of it."[13] Since political aloofness is one of the justifications for the existence of agencies it would be difficult to disagree with Howe.

In many agencies the power to make regulations is "subject to approval of the Governor-in-Council". This veto power of Cabinet is seldom used and in fact isolated incidents, such as the Coyne affair, indicate that neither the Cabinet nor the minister are always consulted or informed about the regulations that have been made even when the regulations are subject to approval of the Cabinet. But the control is available.

The minister through whom the agency reports to Parliament has a number of prerogatives in connection with that agency. Thus the Air Transport Board may issue licenses subject to the approval of the Minister of Transport, "subject to the directions of the Minister the Board shall from time to time make investigations and surveys", and "the Board shall make recommendations to the Minister and advise the Minister".[14] With two exceptions, all agencies report to Parliament through the minister and

---

12 Royal Commission on Government Organization, *op. cit.,* p. 63.
13 *Debates* (Commons) 1946, pp. 2,482-83 as quoted in Hodgetts and Corbett, *op. cit.,* p. 203.
14 Aeronautics Act, Part 11, R.S. 1952, Ch. 2, para. 12.

they are usually required by the founding statute to make an annual report to the minister who is required to table the report in the House.

Most agencies are subject to the provisions of the Financial Administration Act which invokes various financial controls. These controls vary from the whole gamut to which departments are subjected, as in departmental corporations, to the virtual financial autonomy of the proprietary corporations which must submit annual capital budgets but have full banking and borrowing freedom and, so long as no further revenue is required, can act independently except for the requirement to report to the minister as the shareholder. Agency corporations must submit both capital and operating budgets for ministerial approval. The extent of the minister's scrutiny will depend on the minister but is not likely to be in great depth. Most agencies are subject to audit by the Auditor-General which involves more than a purely accounting audit.

As well as being subject to Cabinet controls, the agencies are also responsible to Parliament in varying degrees. Two agencies, the Public Service Commission and the Auditor-General report directly to Parliament in their annual reports although in each case the responsible minister must table the report. The designation of each to a minister makes quite clear that these two agencies, contrary to popular opinion, are subject to some Cabinet supervision. In fact, both agencies have duties for which they are responsible to Cabinet or to individual members of the Cabinet. The Auditor-General has some responsibility to the Minister of Finance and must report to Cabinet through this minister[15] while the Public Service Commission must report directly to Cabinet as it desires or as Cabinet requires and must "perform such other duties and functions with reference to the Public Service as are assigned to it by the Governor-in-Council"[16] in addition to the primary duties listed in the Act. The Commission also has duties for which it is responsible to the Minister of Finance. In the main, however, these two agencies consider themselves responsible to Parliament and not to the government as incorporated in the Cabinet.

Members of Parliament may show their interest in the agencies by asking questions of the minister through whom the agency reports and they will normally get the answer to their questions. Parliament can discuss the affairs of any agency in the general debates such as those which precede the budget debates and if the agency has to ask for Parliamentary appropriations then it expects a discussion of its affairs. The review of agency affairs by Parliamentary committees could be an

---

15 Financial Administration Act, 1951, para. 70(2).
16 Public Service Employment Act, 1967, para. 5 (f).

effective control and Parliament can institute such an investigation at any time. The best known reviews have taken place in the meetings of the Public Accounts Committee.

The government does not lack control devices to measure and regulate the conduct of agencies. These controls are not always used and when exercised affect the general tenor of policy making and not the details of management.

# 5 Bilingualism, Biculturalism, and Senior Public Servants*

## Sylvain Cloutier

A bicultural society is a society within which two communities, two living cultures, remain in a constant state of interaction and cross-fertilization, while each retains its own symbols, priorities, traditions and outlook. It is a society in which each community evolves and matures in its own way, according to its own character. This is our situation in Canada. It is a situation which moves us to seek constantly new ways of ensuring not only the survival but the full development, the full *épanouissement*, of both major cultural groups.

Members of both groups will instinctively continue to look to their governments to deal with the many areas of public policy that have a direct impact on the cultural fabric of the community. There may be differences in outlook and priorities which are likely to colour the positions taken by members of both major cultural groups. Thus, if we wish our political and administrative institutions to reflect the norms and priorities of both groups, we must ensure that representatives from both communities are actively and jointly engaged in the process of policy making and policy implementation at the most senior levels of our public services. We must ensure not only that the representatives of these two communities can communicate with one another but, more important,

* Sylvain Cloutier, "Senior Public Service Officials in a Bicultural Society," *Canadian Public Administration*, Vol. 11, No. 4 (Winter, 1968), pp. 395-406 (reprinted and slightly abridged by permission of author and publisher).

that each can understand and appreciate the other's set of values. Only in this way can our governmental institutions, federal as well as provincial and municipal, acquire sensitivity and responsiveness to the predominant values and priorities within both communities.

Public administrators are all aware of the degree to which governments in the last thirty to forty years have moved from a passive, regulatory role to a positive, action-oriented one, particularly in the social and economic spheres. Aside from the need for specialists required by this transformation, there has also been the need for a new kind of manager, a new kind of public administrator – one who understands the general aspirations of the Canadian people and the broad objectives of government, particularly in the fields of social and economic development. Why is this? Mainly because of the facts of size, complexity, variety and the rapid rate of change that animate government activity today. It is also because senior administrators are policy advisers to their ministers and to the cabinet. Ministers expect that senior administrators will be much more than mere executors of public policy. Because of their often long and close association with certain areas of public policy, because of their real and apparent political impartiality, senior administrators are inevitably also policy planners. And it is particularly in this role that, as a body, their understanding of the social, economic, cultural and political values and aspirations of the Canadian people is most critical. It is in this role also that their awareness and appreciation of cultural differences and similarities and their ability to grasp the cultural perameters within which policy and program orientations are cast by both major groups need to be particularly acute.

Let us not make the mistake of thinking that the answer lies only in proportionate representation of the two groups in our public services – a thing that probably does not exist at this moment in any sizeable public service in the country. Of course proportionate representation will help but, in my view, imbalance in numbers is merely symptomatic of a far more serious and damageable problem – the disequilibrium in the capacity of senior public service officials as a group to comprehend the cultural realities of this country and to give to these cultural realities, in the formulation of policy and the implementation of programs, as much attention as they instinctively give to the social, economic and political implications of proposals.

There are only two ways in which this disequilibrium can be corrected: through qualitative as well as quantitative representation of the two groups at the senior policy levels of public services, and through the acquisition by members of one group, first of an awareness and then of an understanding of the attitudes, the values, the aspirations and the needs of the other group. Only in this way will our public services be bicultural in outlook – and this is urgently needed as, more and more, governments move into areas of public policy that have a profound influence on the cultural fabric of our communities.

So much for the underlying concepts. Let us now look at the pragmatic aspect of the question and ask ourselves how one is to recognize whether or not the senior levels of a public service reflect the cultural realities of Canada.

A useful approach is to look at the representation of each of the two groups among senior public officials, at the incidence, again in each of the two groups, of proficiency in the second official language and finally at whatever programs may exist to increase second language proficiency and to familiarize the members of one group with the culture of the other group. Indeed a prerequisite to understanding another culture is a knowledge of the language in which the nature and dimensions of that culture are defined. For, when all is said and done, before operating bicultural public services, we need to have bilingual public servants.

I wrote to the ten provincial civil service commissions and to the directors of personnel of the twenty largest cities in Canada, asking for any available statistics on the language composition of their public services, for an indication of any existing or contemplated policy or practice relating to the utilization of bilingual public servants, particularly at the senior levels, and for information on any existing or planned language training programs for their public servants. Only in the two cities of Quebec and Montreal is bilingualism considered a factor of selection in all initial appointments and promotions – and progressively so with the level of the position. Only the provinces of New Brunswick and Manitoba reported that they recruited bilingual public servants where service to the community dictated it. And that was it. None of them even mentioned the *senior* levels of their public services; and most equated the French-speaking minority with the other cultural minorities in their area.

Clearly, there exists at most provincial and municipal levels a serious lack of appreciation of one of the basic problems facing our country today. This is not an exaggeration. One to whom I wrote even replied that his associates considered biculturalism as something to do with the two sexes.

Perhaps I am too severe. Admittedly, in the public service of Canada, conditions with respect to the need for bilingualism are unique because we serve all of Canada. Admittedly the other jurisdictions do not face the same requirements and circumstances as we do. Nonetheless it is my deep conviction that no public service in this country can afford to dismiss the issue after only a quick or cursory review, and say "this does not apply to me". It is my conviction that each public service that has not already done so should without delay take full cognizance of the bilingual and bicultural fact of this country and consider seriously the implications of that fact for the Canadians that it serves – even if the Canadians of the second official language minority that it serves number only a handful.

While I am quite prepared to admit that the federal public service still has some distance to go before it can be said to be bilingual in character and bicultural in outlook, let me add immediately that it is well on the way to this goal.

A considerable change has taken place since the days of the old Civil Service Act of 1918, which, until 1961, required that prospective employees speak the language of the majority of the local community in which they were to serve. While this policy could at least be said to constitute a recognition of the bicultural character of the country, it resulted in thousands of citizens not being able to speak their own language when seeking and receiving service from the public service of their country. Not only did this situation, which prevailed until 1962, constitute administrative nonsense, it was also patently unfair.

The Civil Service Act of 1961 adopted a different, more realistic approach. It provided that the language qualifications of employees of local offices should be such that effective service could be given to the public served and that the functions of the offices could be performed adequately.

Following the passage of that legislation, several measures were adopted in succession to ensure that the new policy would be taken into account in the Commission's recruiting programs and that public servants already employed would not be adversely affected by the move towards greater bilingualism in the public service. These measures included the determination of the circumstances in which employees *must* be bilingual, those in which bilingualism would be desirable and would be considered an asset in the assessment of candidates and, finally, the circumstances in which the knowledge of one language only would be required. They included directives on the language composition of selection boards as well as directives on the manner in which second language proficiency was to be recognized as an asset in the assessment of candidates. They included also the launching of special recruitment programs designed to attract greater numbers of French-speaking university graduates to the public service. Finally, they included the opening, in February, 1964, of the first formal Public Service Language School.

The cumulative effect of these measures, together of course with other events that were happening elsewhere in the country, was to bring about a very clear realization on the part of most senior officials that still more had to be done if the public service, and particularly its senior levels, were to be as bicultural in its outlook as the public that it served was in its composition. The crystallization of this attitude quickly led to the development and acceptance by the government of a comprehensive policy on bilingualism and biculturalism in the public service of Canada. In a statement on this policy which he made in the House of Commons on April 6, 1966, Prime Minister Pearson endorsed the measures that had been initiated up to then by the independent Civil Service Commission and went on to announce several new ones that have since been implemented. He also defined the Government's objectives and expectations in this important area in the following words:

> It is the objective of the government to make the Public Service of maximum benefit to the people of Canada by attracting to it the most competent and qualified Canadians available in all parts of Canada. To this end and having regard to the character of our country, the government for several years has been taking practical steps to encourage bilingualism in the Federal Public Service, as part of its fundamental objective of promoting and strengthening national unity on the basis of the equality of rights and opportunities for both English-speaking and French-speaking Canadians. In a diverse federal state, such as Canada, it is important that all citizens should have a fair and equal opportunity to participate in the national administration and to identify themselves with, and feel at home in, their own National Capital.

> The government hopes and expects that, within a reasonable period of years, a state of affairs in the Public Service will be reached whereby

> (a) it will be normal practice for oral or written communications within the service to be made in either official language at the option of the person making them, in the knowledge that they will be understood by those directly concerned;

> (b) communications with the public will normally be in either official language having regard to the person being served;

> (c) the linguistic and cultural values of both English-speaking and French-speaking Canadians will be reflected through civil service recruitment and training; and

> (d) a climate will be created in which public servants from both language groups will work together toward common goals, using their own language and applying their respective cultural values, but each fully understanding and appreciating those of the other.

To underline the importance which he and the Government attached to the implementation of this policy, the Prime Minister announced on the same occasion the establishment within the Privy Council Office of a

Special Secretariat on Bilingualism whose director would be responsible directly to him. This secretariat, working in close consultation and co-operation with the Public Service Commission, the Treasury Board and all deputy ministers and heads of agencies, is responsible for ensuring the co-ordinated and progressive implementation of the Government's policy and program regarding bilingualism in the public service.

The Prime Minister's declaration and the creation of the Special Secretariat, coupled with the passage by Parliament in the spring of 1967 of a new Public Service Employment Act which broadens the statutory base of the Public Service Commission's endeavours to increase the level of bilingualism in the federal public service, have set the stage for several developments of interest.

Our first concern was for the senior public service officials of tomorrow – that is, the new university graduates who enter the public service today. Not only was it decided to consider second official language skills as an element of selection in relation to university graduates applying for administrative and foreign service positions but efforts were redoubled to attract to the public service a greater number of French-speaking candidates. These two measures have paid off handsomely. A growing number of our new university graduate recruits claim some proficiency in both official languages.

Some like to think that it is mostly sophisticated recruitment techniques that have brought about these encouraging results. However, that alone would not have done it. I am convinced that what helped the most was that we did *have* a comprehensive policy on bilingualism in the public service – a policy which satisfied the graduate from French Canada that he could expect to work in his own language, either upon his appointment or at the most within a few years after it, a policy which in the summer of 1967 has sent to language training schools on a full-time basis and for a four-month period as many as 250 of our new university graduate recruits who lacked proficiency either in French or in English.

Largely as a result of these two measures, which there is every intention of continuing, the public service of Canada will be assured, in some fifteen to twenty years from now and permanently thereafter, of sufficient resources from which to appoint truly bilingual senior officials likely to react with greater sensitivity to the cultural outlook of their colleagues.

In the meantime, other measures were needed to produce shorter-term solutions. It is for this reason that language training schools were expanded from the humble beginning in 1964 to the point that we had in the fall of 1967 more than 5,000 public servants engaged in second language training and that plans call for a plateau of about 10,000 students being reached in the year 1971. The 5,000 students, who incidentally were selected on the basis of criteria that gave considerable importance to their level in the government hierarchy, follow one of about ten different types of courses that vary all the way from total immersion for three weeks to one-hour courses each day.

Considerable emphasis is being placed on second language training in order to provide public servants and prospective recruits, to quote from Prime Minister Pearson's statement of April 6, 1966, "with adequate time and opportunity to adapt themselves to new conditions in the service in a way that will increase their own possibilities for a successful and satisfying career".

The "new conditions in the service" to which the Prime Minister referred were mentioned in another part of his policy statement in which he said:
In those centres where a need exists for reasonable proficiency in both languages, procedures will progressively be established for the filling of executive and administrative positions, so that by about 1970 in the case of appointments from outside the service, and by about 1975 in the case of promotions from within, bilingual proficiency or willingness to acquire it, will normally be a requirement for the positions in such centres.

Given the past and projected rate of expansion of our language training schools, most public servants engaged in administrative and executive tasks who want to become bilingual and many others in other occupations will by those dates have had the opportunity of taking language training. Indeed, for the past few months, we have been serving notice on all candidates to administrative and executive positions in centres where bilingualism is desirable, that those appointed are expected to become bilingual if they are not already.

Consequently, we fully expect that, within the next five to ten years present public servants both at the intermediate and senior levels will have acquired a useful degree of proficiency in the second official language. Indeed, our language training programs and our policy of recognizing second language skills as an additional asset in the assessment of candidates have already begun to reap benefits. French is more and more a living language in Ottawa and a number of my French-speaking friends, from both inside and outside the public service, now find that there is more and more a desire to deal with them in their own language, both as a courtesy and as a chance of getting a bit of practice in the newly acquired skill.

At the moment, the public service of Canada is not viewed by *all* Canadians as *their* public service. That is what is wrong with it and that is the situation which the various measures I have described are attempting to correct. I would go on to say: Yes, all of these measures *are* necessary because, in spite of the progress made in recent years, there is still a long way to go. Of the 650 or so most senior officials of the federal public service, only about 100, or 15 per cent, have French as their mother tongue. This represents a considerable increase over the situation which prevailed four or five years ago – the absolute numbers have doubled and the percentage has gone from 12 to 15 – but that is still not adequate representation. Yes, by all means, all these measures are required because, of our 550 or so English-speaking senior officials, it is estimated that about half have no proficiency whatever in the French language, and accordingly little or no understanding of the cultural values that must be reckoned with in the development and implementation of policies and programs that are to serve the whole of Canada.

In conclusion, let me focus again briefly on the role of the senior public service official in our system of government, whether it is at the municipal, provincial or federal level. His role is absolutely of the first order for, in the last analysis, and forgive me for being blunt, he is often in the position of being able to push what he likes or believes in and "block" what he fears or does not like, either at the policy formulation or at the implementation stage. He can do this by his enthusiastic support or his calculated obstruction, by a constructive and positive approach to a problem or by overly-cautious and unimaginative analysis of a proposal and its alternatives, by effective action or by deliberative delay, by forceful and dynamic leadership or by indifferent and uninterested administration.

The importance and complexity of the problems relating to the national life of our country that are facing us today require that nothing be spared to ensure that their consideration, analysis, and resolution are entrusted to the best minds available, working together towards a common solution in a spirit of understanding, respect and trust. I submit that every step taken to increase the bilingual capacity and to broaden the bicultural outlook of the senior officials of any of the public services of this country, banishes some of the insensibility and even the doubts, the fears and the dislikes that unfortunately still exist in some of us and brings us that much closer to that understanding, respect and trust so essential to the promotion of national unity in a greater and stronger Canada.

# 6 Federal-Provincial Administrative Relationships*

## Taylor Cole

The federal bureaucracy has become increasingly involved in the complexities of federal-provincial relationships. These involvements, usually embraced under the heading of cooperative federalism, have injected the federal bureaucracy into the institutional ties in the dynamic federal system. Three factors have, according to Donald V. Smiley, been responsible for the growth of this inter-governmental machinery and relationships.[1] They are: 1) the constitutional rigidities which prompted a search for flexibility through administrative arrangements; 2) the exercise of the powers possessed by the federal government to equalize the range and quality of the public services; and 3) the desire and capacity of administrators at varying levels of responsibility to "devise and implement collaboration arrangements." Whatever be the relative weight placed upon each of these explanations, there has developed a myriad and rapidly increasing number of committees and meetings which play a key part in these cooperative arrangements.

Three types of inter-governmental machinery, which have come into being, can be differentiated on the basis of the degree of the federal

* Taylor Cole, *The Canadian Bureaucracy and Federalism 1947-1965*, Graduate School of International Studies (Denver, University of Denver Press, 1966) (reprinted by permission of author and publisher).
[1] Donald V. Smiley, "Public Administration and Canadian Federalism", *Canadian Public Administration*, Vol. 7 (September, 1964), pp. 372-73. Professor Smiley prefers to speak of "joint federalism" and "consultative federalism", rather than cooperative federalism.

initiative in their establishment, the part played by federal officials in their operation, and the territorial areas which are involved. The one type of committee and meeting has come into being generally at federal initiative, finds its headquarters or secretariat as a rule in Ottawa, and involves functions in the federal-provincial area where federal and provincial governments usually have concurrent jurisdiction. These committees and meetings, that is, the formal as distinguished from the informal ones, were the subject of a study by K. W. Taylor, then Deputy Minister of Finance, in 1958.[2] At that time, he found some 67 "federal-provincial committees," 14 of which had broad and 50 narrow "terms of reference." These committees included 5 which were operating at the ministerial level, 13 at the deputy minister level, 18 at the director level, and 28 at the professional and technical level. Membership in 40 of these consisted of governmental personnel, whereas the membership of 24 included non-governmental personnel. The secretaries of all except half a dozen of these committees and meetings were federal officials.

Since Taylor made this pioneering study eight years ago the committee structure has become much more complex. Two closely cooperating centers of influence in Ottawa, the Prime Minister's Office and the Ministry of Finance, are heavily involved. The functions of the Federal-Provincial Relations Division in the Ministry of Finance, which was created in 1954, have grown in a number of ways in connection with the meetings of the Federal-Provincial Conferences. The Assistant Deputy Minister, who heads this Division, is a key participant, and along with the Deputy Minister of Finance is active in the work of the Continuing Committee on Fiscal and Economic Matters of the Federal-Provincial Conference. These two officials also play key roles in the work of the Tax Structure Committee of the Federal-Provincial Conference. The Tax Structure Committee is composed of the federal and provincial ministers of finance, or their ministerial counterparts, and is preparing studies on which projections for tax sharing, equalization, and inter-governmental fiscal relationships for the period from 1967-1972 can be based. As previously indicated, the federal Cabinet has a special committee on federal-provincial relations whose special secretariat maintains liaison with the appropriate officials in the provinces and federal ministries. He prepares the agenda and attends the meetings of Federal-Provincial Conferences. Thus, important new machinery has been recently established or expanded in the office of the Prime Minister and Ministry of Finance to cope with the growing complexities of federal-provincial relations.

2 K. W. Taylor, "Co-ordination in Administration", in J. E. Hodgetts and D. C. Corbett, *Canadian Public Administration* (Toronto, The Macmillan Company of Canada Limited, 1960), pp. 145-64 (including discussion by R. B. Bryce).

But perhaps more important has been the rapid expansion of the federal-provincial committees and meetings, and especially those dealing with professional and technical problems. By the end of 1964, the number of Federal-Provincial Conferences, committees, and other meetings had nearly doubled since 1957 to a total of 114.[3] Twenty of these were at the ministerial level. Some 62, or approximately half of them, involved participation by all provinces, whereas the balance involved only the federal government and one or more provinces. The "authority" for the meetings ranged from decisions of Federal-Provincial Conferences, to federal statute, to federal Order-In-Council, to action by the Cabinet, to federal departmental "initiative," and, in a few cases, to "provincial sponsorship." The federal representation on the purely professional and technical conferences and meetings, as was to be expected, has been the heaviest from the Ministries of Health and Welfare, Agriculture, Forestry, and Labour. The importance of these meetings ranges from that of the Federal-Provincial Conferences and its Tax Structure Committee to that of such "meetings" as those on Ownership of Beds of Pre-Confederation Harbours and on the Replacement of Swing Bridges and Canal Systems. Several of these meetings, such as the ones on Provincial Taxation of Joint Canada-United States Defence Projects and on Cultural Agreements with France and Belgium, have external affairs implications.

The contributions of the federal officials in providing much of the leadership, administrative direction, and implementation of decisions are recognized in many quarters. The personal testimony of participating officials in provincial capitals, including Quebec, is one bit of evidence. Competent students, such as Donald V. Smiley, conclude that the program specialists from the bureaucracy have removed certain types of decision-making from the political arena and have produced an impressive amount of non-controversial agreement.[4] The Glassco Commission found that there were no less than 16 federal departments and an equal number of agencies, which now "have some close and significant concern with matters in which provincial governments had common or related interests" and that "the points of intersecting interest" had multiplied.[5]

---

[3] (Editor's Note) *The Calendar of Federal-Provincial Conferences and Meetings—1967* listed 121 conferences or meetings. The frequency with which these groups met during 1967 ranged from annually through "every other month" to "as required". Eleven of the conferences were ministerial and eighty involved participants from all provinces.

[4] Smiley, *op. cit.*, pp. 378-79; see, by the same author, *Conditional Grants and Canadian Federalism* (Toronto, Canadian Tax Foundation, 1963), p. 38.

[5] Royal Commission on Government Organization, Vol. 3 (Ottawa, Queen's Printer, 1962), p. 124; see also A. R. Kear, "Co-operative Federalism: A Study of the Federal-Provincial Continuing Committee on Fiscal and Economic Matters," *Canadian Public Administration,* Vol. 6 (March, 1963), p. 56.

It concluded that added responsibilities and staff should be given to the Division of Federal-Provincial Relations to advise in general regarding federal-provincial consultative and cooperative arrangements, and, specifically, regarding consultation, conditional grants, administrative delegation, and contracting services by one government for another.

Despite this accumulating evidence, the full appraisal of the role of the federal official in this rapidly growing network of federal-provincial committees and meetings must still be based somewhat on subjective evaluations, at least, until, as J. E. Hodgetts suggests, the need for more "full scale studies of provincial services . . . and of the administrative interrelations which have developed between provincial and federal public departments"[6] has been satisfied. Until that time, we shall not be able to evaluate the collaborative and competitive relationships and to compare the contributions of the federal-provincial meetings of the federal officials with those of the increasing number of able and active provincial officials who are participating.[7]

On the horizontal level, where the initiative has been taken by the provincial governments, where the emphasis is upon the provinces and inter-provincial relationships as such, and where the federal official is less in evidence, the growth of committees and meetings has also been rapid since World War II. In the first major study made of "inter-provincial co-operation" in 1958, Richard H. Leach found a surprisingly large number of professional and technical meetings and organizations which were composed partially or exclusively of public officials from the provinces.[8] The purely inter-provincial meetings have often invited federal officials as observers, or even as members, and the nature of their participation has depended upon the circumstances. There is no constitu-

---

6 J. E. Hodgetts, "Challenge and Response", *Canadian Public Administration*, Vol. 7 (December, 1964), p. 411.

7 "My own impression," says one highly capable critic, "is that the increasing frequency and importance of federal-provincial meetings is bringing about a community of sorts . . . [through] Bryce, Kent, and especially Johnson from Ottawa, Morin from Quebec, MacDonald (newly-appointed Chief Economist from Ontario), Tansley from New Brunswick, and possibly Veitch from British Columbia." The new channels of communication between Ottawa and the provincial capitals, says another observer, are "between the civil services of both governments". This development can be explained in the case of Quebec by the rise of a "new group and mentality within the Quebec civil service [many of whom have come from the federal civil service] which corresponds more closely to the type of men and patterns of thinking in the Ottawa civil service". Peter Desbarats, *The State of Quebec* (Toronto, McClelland and Stewart, 1965), p. 134.

8 Richard H. Leach, "Inter-provincial Co-operation: Neglected Aspects of Canadian Federalism," *Canadian Public Administration*, Vol. 2 (June, 1959), pp. 83-99. It is to be noted that the Province of Quebec has established a special Department of Federal-Provincial Relations.

tional basis for inter-provincial cooperation as such, but its development has an important bearing on the contours of Canadian federalism.

Two recent examples of such meetings at quite different levels of participation have been the annual inter-provincial Premiers' conferences which were revived on the initiative of Quebec in 1960. One federal official was present at the first meeting in strictly an observer capacity. Again, the meeting of presidents or chairmen of civil service commissions was started in 1963, with Quebec again taking some initiative. A secretariat has been established for the exchange of information, and the annual meetings have been attended by commissioners and invited officials from the Public Service Commission in Ottawa. The province of Saskatchewan was reported in 1960 to be represented in some capacity in at least 75 organizations where inter-provincial cooperation was a matter of major concern, though, as J. H. Aitchison has pointed out, there was "federal representation" on nearly all of them.[9]

Looming on the horizon are the organizations which have a distinctive area orientation. Already many of the federal-provincial and inter-provincial committees and meetings are largely constituted of members from regional areas, such as the Maritimes, to deal with problems of coordination at regional levels.[10] The growth of municipal governments and of metropolitan areas has prompted discussion of three-tier and three-level federalism[11] and of a real division of powers.[12] Proposals for regional levels of government receive academic mention,[13] and the Glassco Commission was concerned with appraisals of future dispersion of operations.[14] Regional concerns receive special attention in the presentation of party and provincial government programs.[15]

---

[9] J. H. Aitchison, "Interprovincial Co-operation in Canada," *The Political Process in Canada* (Toronto, University of Toronto Press, 1963), esp. pp. 165-66.

[10] See, for example, Hon. Maurice Sauvé, "Problems of Regional Development in Canada," *Professional Public Service,* Vol. 43 (October, 1964), pp. 2-4.

[11] Note the criticism of the inadequacy of the "normal federal-provincial channels to serve the interests of municipal governments" in George S. Mooney, "The Canadian Federation of Mayors and Municipalities: Its Role and Functions," *Canadian Public Administration,* Vol. 3 (March, 1960), pp. 82-92, esp. pp. 86-87. This is not a new point of view.

[12] J. Stefan Dupré, "Applied Areal Analysis: The Case of Canada," in Arthur Maas, ed., *Area and Power* (New York, The Free Press, 1959), pp. 89-109.

[13] Eric Beecroft, "Agenda for Regional Government," *Canadian Public Administration,* Vol. 5 (June, 1962), pp. 227-28.

[14] Royal Commission on Government Organization, Vol. 5 (1963), pp. 79ff.

[15] Note, for example, J. W. Pickersgill, *The Liberal Party* (Toronto, McClelland and Stewart, 1962), pp. 125-26. For a discussion of the matters being considered at the sixth Premiers' conference in Winnipeg in 1965, see *Winnipeg Free Press* (August 3, 1965), p. 1.

Whatever be the direction and rapidity of these developments, federal-provincial, inter-provincial, or regional, the handiwork of the federal public employees is present in some capacity at nearly every stage. Their involvements give both added flexibility and additional strength to the complex of flexible and dynamic interrelationships which constitute the heart of the federal system in Canada.

# 7 The Secretariat of the Constitutional Conference<sup>*</sup>

## Edgar Gallant

At a meeting in February 1968, the First Ministers of the federal and the ten provincial governments set up a Constitutional Conference on a continuing basis to supervise the process of reviewing the Canadian Constitution. A Continuing Committee of Officials, composed of senior public servants from the federal and provincial governments, was established to assist the Conference.[1] The Conference also provided for the formation of a Secretariat to serve both the Constitutional Conference and the Continuing Committee of Officials.[2]

In recent years, the federal government has usually provided some secretariat services to the surprisingly wide range of consultative bodies

---

* Edgar Gallant, "A New Framework for Constitutional Review," (reprinted and abridged by permission of author). This selection is part of an address delivered to the Toronto Regional Group of the Institute of Public Administration of Canada on January 22, 1969. It focuses on that part of the address concerned with "the intergovernmental secretariat."

1 It was decided that the Continuing Constitutional Conference and its Continuing Committee should examine the questions of official languages, fundamental rights, distribution of powers, reform of institutions linked with federalism (including the Senate and the Supreme Court of Canada), regional disparities, amending procedures and provisional arrangements, and mechanisms of federal-provincial relations.

2 Since this article was prepared, the second meeting of the Constitutional Conference took place from February 10 to 12, 1969. The Conference decided, among other things, to establish a number of additional ministerial committees, which are also to be served by the Secretariat.

which have been developed for purposes of federal-provincial liaison. The idea has been increasingly advanced that a full-time secretariat of a continuing and intergovernmental nature is now required, at least for the highest level of federal-provincial consultation and negotiation where the key policy items are considered. The continuing nature of the secretariat is needed because of the complexity of modern government and the extent to which policies of both levels of government impinge upon one another. The intergovernmental nature is necessary to ensure objectivity in the services being rendered to consultative bodies.

An intergovernmental secretariat in the "pure" sense would be a body responsible to the eleven governments jointly, with the Secretary reporting to the consultative body concerned (say the Federal-Provincial Conference of Prime Ministers and Premiers) with its costs shared by the eleven governments on the basis of some formula, and its program and practices subject to the agreement of the participating governments.

The problems associated with a "pure" intergovernmental secretariat, however, are these:

1. The secretariat would in effect be a public service body, maintained with public funds, but not directly accountable to an electorate through one democratically elected Parliament or Legislature. If the will of the people with respect to this expenditure of public funds had to be expressed through eleven elected bodies at the same time, difficulties would be created for our traditional concepts of responsible government. This would not be an issue of practical significance for a relatively small and temporary service unit to a conference but could be extremely significant for a permanent secretariat, particularly if the secretariat exercised executive or advisory functions.

2. A related problem is that federal-provincial bodies do not normally come to decisions because the delegates are ultimately accountable to their own governments or legislatures and cannot give firm commitments at a conference. Thus, conferences seek to arrive at a conclusion or a concensus which might later be reflected in executive or legislative action. A sense of unanimity is sought without resorting to a formal vote. When there is no sense of agreement, governments may have to take unilateral action within their own jurisdiction while being aware of course of the viewpoints of other governments. To function effectively, the intergovernmental secretariat would probably require some definite decisions with respect to its operations, so that it could not always rely for proper direction on the informal concensus approach. But if a "board of directors" approach were to be considered, the problem of allocating voting would be difficult. Would it be legitimate, for example, to simply allocate

one vote per participating government, when some provinces are much larger than others and when the federal government represents more voters than all the provincial governments put together?

3. As a share of such a secretariat's budget would be obtained from each of the participating governments, the secretariat could be paralyzed into inaction if it were subjected to budgetary and control procedures of eleven different governments.

While various practical accommodations could no doubt be found to overcome these specific problems, a strictly intergovernmental secretariat clearly could involve a significant change in our machinery for intergovernmental relations, and could raise some questions concerning our traditional concepts of the proper exercise of political processes in Canada.

The Constitutional Conference Secretariat is not at present an intergovernmental secretariat in this "pure" sense. The Secretariat was set up as a special unit attached for administrative purposes to the federal government but pains have been taken to develop an objectivity both in appearance and in fact. Although the administrative connection to the Privy Council Office exists, the Secretariat operates autonomously as far as its work program is concerned. The Secretary is guided by the policy direction given by the Constitutional Conference and the Continuing Committee of Officials; between meetings, he frequently consults members of the Committee by telephone or by visits to provincial capitals. He must also seek the views of the Chairman of the Conference or of the Committee. It has been agreed that, while the Secretariat cannot become a policy advisor to any government in particular, the Secretary of the Conference and members of his staff must be kept informed on developments and attitudes in all governments. Also, the objectivity and breadth of view of the Secretariat will be increased through the secondment of provincial officials for a tour of duty with the Secretariat. The Constitutional Conference Secretariat, then, represents something of a compromise between the "pure" intergovernmental secretariat and the former practice of the provision of services by the federal government.

The existing responsibilities of the Secretariat are as follows:

1. The execution of a number of administrative functions such as

(a) overseeing the physical arrangements for the various meetings, involving such matters as the layout of the meeting room, the provision of appropriate papers, simultaneous interpretation services, secretarial services, security, and press, radio, and television arrangements.

(b) preparing a summary record of the proceedings of all in-camera meetings of the Conference and its committees or sub-committees.

Since intergovernmental meetings are not decision-making sessions in the usual sense of the term, the Secretariat does not try to produce a "record of decisions". Rather, it aims for an analytical summary which identifies and describes as concisely as possible the main items of discussion and gives a balanced interpretation of the views expressed or implied by the various delegations. This is one of the important ways by which the Secretariat facilitates intergovernmental dialogue.

(c) ensuring that required follow-up occurs after meetings. An orderly flow of reports and information must take place between the Conference and its committees. Provision must also be made for orderly administration of documentation relating to the constitutional review.

2. The performance of special functions, which might be assigned by the Constitutional Conference or the Continuing Committee. These tasks could include various analyses of documentation, the preparation of background or factual studies, and the coordination of other studies needed on various subjects. Obviously, the Secretariat should not do research leading to precise conclusions about broad policy matters. Such conclusions could undermine a particular government's position based on different but perhaps equally valid considerations. The Secretariat must be the servant of all the governments.

3. The fulfillment of a liaison function. The Secretariat could act in a kind of quasi-diplomatic role by serving as a source of communication and interpretation to facilitate the development of understanding between governments. It could provide a continuing link among members of the committees between meetings. If the Secretariat is kept well informed on developments and attitudes within all governments, it should also be able to help prevent misunderstandings and enable governments to take into account views and aspirations in other parts of the country when developing their own positions.

# 8 Personnel Management in the Federal Public Service*

## R. H. Dowdell

## *The Influence of the Political Environment*

Despite broad and growing similarities, personnel management in the public service is different in many ways from its counterpart in the private sector. One of the principal differences can be identified at the highest level in government organization. In the public service, the concept of management must include the political heads of departments – i.e., the ministers of the Crown. It is commonly thought that the deputy minister – the senior appointed official under the minister – is the top management official in the department, but reference to any of the Acts of Parliament establishing government departments will dispel this notion. For example, section 22(1) of the Government Organization Act (1966) reads as follows:

> The Minister of Forestry and Rural Development holds office during pleasure and has the management and direction of the Department of Forestry and Rural Development.

If the Minister is a manager, he is also a politician. Indeed, perhaps first and foremost a politician, for he will not remain a minister for long unless he can get elected to Parliament, be re-elected whenever the occa-

---

* R. H. Dowdell, "Personnel Administration in the Federal Public Service," in A. M. Willms and W. D. K. Kernaghan, *Public Administration in Canada* (Toronto, Methuen Publications, 1968), pp. 360-88 (reprinted and abridged by permission of author and publisher).

51

sion demands, and exercise considerable political skill in executing his portion of the government's program.

In a commercial enterprise, the product or service must be produced at a profit. In the long run, there must be prospects of a reasonable rate of return on investment to bring the business into being and ensure its continued existence. The profit criterion is at once an important motive underlying plans, policies and decisions, and a yardstick against which their effectiveness can be assessed. Personnel directors in the private sector are in general agreement that one of their chief objectives is to contribute to their firms' profitability.

The pervasive characteristic of the public service is political rather than commercial. The administrator in the public service implements public policies and programs which have been shaped by political forces. His superiors are politicians – leaders of a political party or coalition which obtained, if not a majority, at least the largest number of seats in the House of Commons because it convinced the electorate it had the best program and was best qualified to carry it out. These elected executives will tend to do the things likely to ensure their re-election and to avoid doing things which jeopardize it. The public service is subject to their direction and accountable to them. They in turn are accountable to Parliament for the conduct of the public service and not the least of the senior public servant's concerns is to avoid embarrassing his minister. Thus the political criterion is to the public service what the profit criterion is to industry – the thread which runs through the decision-making pro‐cess, and the standard against which these decisions must ultimately be weighed. That is not to say that every action must be calculated for the political advantage of the party in power any more than every action in business must be calculated to maximize profit. Short-run disadvan‐tages must sometimes be borne and there are many actions whose political consequences are too remote to affect decisions significantly. But in the long-run, top management of the public service must on balance redound to the credit of the party in power and in the short-run, actions which may produce adverse political consequences must be avoided as much as possible.

If these considerations are true of management generally in the public service, they are equally true of personnel management in particular. In a commercial organization, personnel policies and actions are evaluated by the profit criterion. The political criterion, however, is a nebulous thing at best and less susceptible to objective estimate. It is more likely to be applied by evaluating the sum of immediate consequences arising out of policies and actions. There is a temptation to regard each personnel action as an opportunity to secure a return of political advantage and to avoid those which are politically dangerous. For example, before the reform of the Canadian public service it was generally accepted that the party in power would use its power of appointment to secure or reward political support and the opponents of reform argued that a government must be able to depend on the loyalty of those who administer its policies.

Whatever may be said in theory for personnel practices based on short or long-term political advantage, the results were generally unfortunate. Although political appointees were sometimes people of great ability (MacKenzie King got his start in the public service as a patronage appointee), it was generally true that their qualifications for the job in question were a secondary consideration and frequently even minimum standards of ability were disregarded altogether. Security of tenure was uncertain and few political appointees tended to regard the public service as a career. The inevitable result was a low standard of competence and a poor quality of service to the public. At a time when government activity was highly circumscribed by today's standards, this situation could be tolerated. However, as the activities of the government began to expand, it became more and more necessary to employ people with the highest possible level of technical and administrative ability. To achieve this, methods of appointment and conditions of employment had to be changed.

## The Merit Principle and Merit Systems

The merit principle which has replaced the patronage system as one of the cornerstones of personnel policy in the public service is an attempt to abandon political considerations altogether in managing the human resources of the public service. The significance of this policy may not be readily appreciated. To take politics out of public personnel management is to run counter to the very nature of the public service as an organization established to pursue political objectives. However necessary such a course may be, it generates stresses which are comparable to the psychological effects of repression. The political character of the public service which is denied outward expression in personnel management is nonetheless at the root of many of its problems, and accounts for many of its inconsistencies and shortcomings. One of the criteria by which public personnel management must be judged is its ability to cope with this dualism in its own character.

The merit principle is really two interrelated principles:

1. Canadian citizens should have a reasonable opportunity to be considered for employment in the public service

2. Selections must be based exclusively on merit, or fitness to do the job.

These principles are among the most important goals of policy in public personnel management. The merit *system* is the mechanism in use at any given time by which these goals are achieved. The merit principle has become, and should remain, a relatively stable part of our public ethic, although like all ethical tenets it may suffer somewhat in practice. A merit system is an administrative device which can and should be adapted to changing circumstances.

## Some Aspects of Organization

The relationships involved in the development and implementation of personnel policy in the Canadian public service have been compared to a triangle, comprising the Treasury Board, the departments and the Public Service Commission. The first two are part of the management structure whereas the third is not. Yet the Commission has had a prominent – indeed until recently the pre-eminent – role in this three-way partnership. In 1966, Parliament passed three pieces of legislation which were proclaimed in force in March, 1967:

1. the Public Service Employment Act (replacing the Civil Service Act)
2. amendments to the Financial Administration Act
3. the Public Service Staff Relations Act.

All three had a bearing on the future role of the Commission. The first established a Public Service Commission to regulate staffing in the portion of the public service over which the former Civil Service Commission had jurisdiction. In addition, prevailing rate employees and ships' crews, previously exempt, were brought under the Act and provision was made to extend it by Order-in-Council to other parts of the service. The amendments to the Financial Administration Act transferred responsibility for position classification to the Treasury Board. The Public Service Staff Relations Act included terms which made the new Public Service Staff Relations Board responsible for pay research and for hearing grievances on disciplinary matters which were previously the subject of appeals to the Commission.

## Improvements in Career Planning

Manpower inventories have been established or are in the process of being established for most of the occupational groups in the administrative and foreign service category, and studies are under way to apply similar methods in the scientific and professional, and technical categories. These techniques can facilitate staff development and career planning, but other important measures must also be taken. Some of these have been incorporated in recent legislative and procedural changes in the public service.

1. The right of employees to appeal the lateral movement of another employee from one position to another at the same salary level was eliminated in the Public Service Employment Act of 1967. This removed a formidable barrier to the mobility of the work force.

2. In certain occupations, notably personnel and financial administration, it is now accepted that the stage on which an employee's career role will be played is service-wide and the tendency to limit careers to a single department is being overcome.

3. Career-planning guidelines are being established on a trial basis for certain occupations and the lessons learned will enable improvements to be made when similar guidelines are developed for other occupations. These guidelines endeavour to balance management and employee interests under a rational staffing policy which permits planned assignments, varied experience, periodical consideration for promotion, and a reduction of raiding between departments.

4. Manpower planning and development is now recognized as a sub-specialization of the personnel function and provision for its exercise is being made in the organization of the Treasury Board and departments. This function includes organization planning, the analysis of manpower requirements, employee evaluation, and training and development.

5. Long-term staff development programs such as the recently announced Career Assignment Program are being introduced. These programs include formal training and planned work assignments lasting several years, requiring the assumption of responsibility and the achievement of results fully commensurate with the employee's salary level. They are primarily a departmental responsibility within policy guidelines set by central management. And they use the facilities of the Public Service Commission to supplement departmental training resources and to effect interdepartmental assignments.

6. Financial barriers to interregional mobility are being reduced by compensating employees for some of the cost of buying and selling homes, and for incidental expenses which were not previously admissible under the travel and removal regulations.

7. Rules governing in-grade salary increases have been altered in a number of classes to permit more appropriate recognition of superior performance. Instead of the one-increase-a-year which became virtually

automatic, deputy ministers can now grant increases of varying amounts, depending on the calibre of an officer's work in relation to that of his peers. Performance pay budgets have been designed in such a way that larger increases for the best performers must be balanced by smaller increases or none at all for others. Varying forms of performance pay are now applicable in the executive category, the upper two or three levels of the administrative and foreign service category, and in the research scientist class. Similar plans will probably be instituted for other scientific and professional classes, and perhaps also for lower levels in the administrative and foreign service category.

## *Training*

Training is the process through which an employee acquires the knowledge, skills and attitudes required to make him fully effective in doing his job. Along with other techniques, such as planned work assignments, it is one of the elements in his development toward positions of greater responsibility. The public service has a particularly great demand for training of all kinds. It employs a greater variety of occupational skills than any other organization, including many that are unique to government. Like all employers, it must cope with rapid technological change. And the service it provides to the public is subject to frequent change, sometimes on short notice, because of the introduction of new government programs.

Training activities in the public service are so extensive and varied that a book could be devoted to their cataloguing. For example, in addition to the induction, skill, supervisory and management training found in all larger organizations, government must train *ab initio* in a number of highly complex fields such as air traffic control and meteorology. It must adapt basic professional skills in engineering and accounting to unique job requirements in purchasing and contract administration. As the largest employer of physical, biological and social scientists in the country, it sponsors post-graduate education for several hundred employees each year. In recent years it has undertaken the massive task of training thousands of employees to serve the public in both official languages.

The Treasury Board is responsible for training policy in the public service and for determining the resources to be allocated for this purpose. Most training programs are administered by the departments. The Public Service Commission interprets its mandate in staffing to include all measures required to meet the needs of the service for qualified personnel. Its Training and Development Branch conducts courses in administrative and managerial skills which are common to all departments and will assist them in developing training programs of their own.

# 9 Financial Administration in Canada*

## H. R. Balls

The financial affairs of the Government of Canada are administered and controlled under the fundamental principles that no tax shall be imposed and no money shall be spent without the authority of Parliament and that expenditures shall be made only for the purposes authorized by Parliament. The most important constitutional provisions relating to Parliament's control of finances are contained in the British North America Act; this Act provides that all federal taxing and appropriating measures must originate in the House of Commons and all requests for grants must come from the Crown through responsible Ministers, and for such requests the Government is solely responsible. In practice, financial control is exercised through a budgetary system based on the principle that all the financial needs of the Government for each fiscal year be considered at one time so that both the current condition and the prospective condition of the public treasury are clearly in evidence.

## Estimates and Appropriations

The co-ordination of the Estimates process is carried out by the Treasury Board. This Board is a separate department of government, its Minister

* H. R. Balls, "Financial Administration in Canada," in *Canada Year Book 1968* (Ottawa, Queen's Printer, 1968), pp. 123-27 (reprinted by permission of author and publisher). This article was written in consultation with D. R. Yeomans of the Treasury Board. The editor extends appreciation to Mr. Balls for his work in updating this selection.

having the designation of President of the Treasury Board. In addition to the President, the Board consists of the Minister of Finance, who serves ex officio as a member, and four other Privy Councillors. Under the Financial Administration Act, the Board may act for the Privy Council in all matters relating to financial management including estimates, expenditures, financial commitments, establishments, revenues, accounts, terms and conditions of employment of persons in the public service and general administrative policy in the public service.

The Estimates for any one fiscal year are determined as a result of a two-phased review by the Treasury Board of departmental proposals for expenditure. In the spring of each year, at the request of the Secretary of the Treasury Board, each department submits to the Treasury Board a forecast of Estimates for the current and following four fiscal years. During the summer, a review of the programs giving rise to these Estimates forecasts is carried out by the Treasury Board, as a result of which tentative Estimates figures are determined for each department for the coming fiscal year. The Board reviews each departmental program submission in the light of probable revenues and governmental policy generally, usually consulting the appropriate Minister and officials. Each department, using the figure resulting from this review as a guideline, develops in detail its manpower and other resource requirements and submits them to the Treasury Board late in October in the form of Main Estimates for the fiscal year beginning the following April 1. These Estimates are analysed by the Treasury Board staff and compared with the guidelines determined during the spring program review. The Board reviews each departmental submission in the light of the current budgetary outlook. The Estimates may be rejected or reduced and unresolved differences of opinion may be referred to the Cabinet for decision. When the Board is satisfied with their substance and form, the Main Estimates are submitted to the Cabinet and later to the Governor in Council for approval and are then laid before the House of Commons.

On motion of the President of the Privy Council, the Estimates of each department are initially referred for consideration to the appropriate standing committee of the House on or before March 1. Under the standing orders of the House, the committees are to report by May 31. The Government House Leader must give forty-eight hours notice of a motion for the House to concur in the Estimates that have been considered by the committees. The consideration of the Estimates usually extends over a period of several months. Each vote is the subject of a separate resolution and Members of the House may question the Minister on any item but no private member or Minister on his own responsibility can introduce any new expenditure proposal or any amendment to an Estimates item that would result in an increased expenditure. When the examination of the individual items has been completed, a resolution approving the granting of moneys is referred to a committee of the whole House. When such resolutions are passed, an appropriation Bill is introduced which, when approved by the House of Commons and the Senate, is given Royal Assent and becomes law. Grants in the Appropriation Acts are grants to the Crown and funds cannot be disbursed until the supply voted by Parliament to the Crown is released by a warrant prepared on an Order of the Governor in Council and signed by the Governor General.

As weeks or months may elapse after the commencement of the fiscal year before the main Appropriation Act is passed, funds are made available for the conduct of government functions by the passage of an interim supply Bill granting one or more twelfths of the total of each item in the Estimates. Additional interim supply Bills may be introduced if required, awaiting Parliament's detailed consideration of the Estimates. In addition, to cover any new and unforeseen requirements that might arise during the year, Supplementary Estimates may be introduced, and just prior to the end of the fiscal year further Supplementary Estimates are laid before the House. These Supplementary Estimates are dealt with in the same manner as the Main Estimates.

In addition to the expenditure items included in the annual Appropriation Acts, there are a number of items such as interest on the public debt, family allowances, and old age assistance payments, which have been authorized under the provisions of other statutes. Although it is not necessary for Parliament to pass annually on these items, they are included in the Main Estimates for purposes of information. Statutory provision also exists for the expenditure of public money in emergencies where no parliamentary appropriation is available. Under the Financial Administration Act, the Governor in Council, upon the report of the President of the Treasury Board that there is no appropriation for the expenditure and upon the report of the appropriate Minister that the expenditure is urgently required, may order the issuance of a special warrant authorizing disbursement of the amount required. Such warrants may be issued only when Parliament is not in session, and every warrant must be published in the *Canada Gazette* within thirty days of issue and reported to Parliament within fifteen days of assembly. The Fire Losses Replacement Account Act also provides for emergency expenditures for the urgent repair or replacement of property destroyed or damaged by fire, where there is not sufficient money available in the appropriation for the Service suffering loss. Such amounts must be charged subsequently to an appropriation or included in the Estimates for the Department or agency concerned.

In addition, disbursements are made for purposes not reflected in the budgetary accounts but recorded in the Government's statement of assets and liabilities, such as loans to and investments in Crown corporations, loans to international organizations and to national, provincial and municipal governments, and loans to veterans. There are also disbursements in connection with deposit and trust accounts and annuity, insurance and pension accounts which the Government holds or administers, including the old age security fund and the Canada Pension Plan fund which are operated as separate entities. Although these disbursements are excluded from the calculation of the annual budgetary surplus or deficit, they are all subject to appropriation by Parliament either in the annual Appropriation Acts or in other legislation.

## *The Budget*

Some time after the Main Estimates have been introduced, the Minister of Finance presents his annual Budget Speech in the House of Commons. Budget papers, tabled for the information of Parliament at least one day prior to the presentation of the Budget, include a general review of economic conditions and a preliminary review of the Government's accounts for the fiscal year then ending. The Budget Speech itself reviews the state of the national economy and the financial operations of the Government for the previous fiscal year and gives a forecast of the probable financial requirements for the year ahead, taking into account the Main Estimates and making allowances for Supplementary Estimates and probable lapsings. At the close of his address, the Minister tables the formal resolutions for changes in the existing tax rates and customs tariff which, in accordance with parliamentary procedure, must precede the introduction of any money Bills. These resolutions give notice of the amendments which the Government intends to ask Parliament to make in the taxation statutes. However, if a change is proposed in a commodity tax, such as a sales tax or excise duty on a particular item, it is usually made effective immediately; the legislation, when passed, is made retroactive to the date of the Speech.

The Budget Speech is delivered in support of a motion that the House go into committee, the debate on which may take up six sitting days. With the passage of the motion, the way is clear for the consideration of the Budget resolutions and, when these have been approved by the Committee, a report to this effect is made to the House and the tax Bills are introduced and thereafter dealt with in the same manner as all other government financial legislation.

# Revenues and Expenditures

The administrative procedures whereby revenues are collected and expenditures are made are, for the most part, contained in the Financial Administration Act.

With respect to revenues, the basic requirement is that all public money shall be paid into the Consolidated Revenue Fund, which is defined as the aggregate of all public money on deposit to the credit of the Receiver General. Under the Government Organization Act of 1969, the Minister of Supply and Services is the Receiver General for Canada. The Treasury Board has prescribed detailed regulations governing the receipts and deposit of such money. For the actual custody of public money, use is made of the Bank of Canada and the chartered banks. Balances are allocated to the various chartered banks on the basis of a percentage allocation established by agreement among all the banks and communicated to the Department of Finance by the Canadian Bankers' Association. The daily operating account is maintained with the Bank of Canada and the division of funds between it and the chartered banks takes into account the immediate cash requirements of the Government and consideration of monetary policy. The Minister of Finance may purchase and hold securities of, or guaranteed by, Canada and pay for them out of the Consolidated Revenue Fund or may sell such securities and pay the proceeds into the Fund. Thus, if cash balances in the Fund are in excess of requirements for the immediate future they may be invested in interest-earning assets. In addition, the Minister of Finance has established a purchase fund to assist in the orderly retirement of the public debt.

The Treasury Board exercises detailed central control over the budgets, programs and staffs of departments and over financial and administrative matters generally. Although the most important part of this control function is exercised during the annual consideration of departmental long-range program plans and the Estimates, the Board maintains continuous control over certain types of expenditure to ensure that the scale of activities and commitments for the future is held within approved policies, that departments follow uniform, efficient and economical practices, and that the Government is informed of and approves any major development of policy or significant transaction that might give rise to public or parliamentary criticism.

To ensure that the decisions of Parliament, the Government, and Ministers – in regard to expenditures – are enforced, the Financial Administration Act provides that no payment shall be made out of the Consolidated Revenue Fund without the authority of Parliament, and no charge shall be made against an appropriation except upon the requisition of the appropriate Minister or a person authorized by him in writing. These requisitions, and certificates that the work has been performed, the material supplied or the services rendered and that the price charged is reasonable or according to contract, together with such documents as may be required, are presented to the Receiver General who makes the payment.

At the beginning of each fiscal year each department submits to the Treasury Board a division into allotments of each vote included in its Estimates. Once approved by the Board, these allotments cannot be varied or amended without the approval of the Board and expenditures charged to appropriations are limited to such allotments. To avoid over-expenditures within a fiscal year, commitments coming in course of payment within the year for which Parliament has provided or has been asked to provide appropriations are recorded and controlled by the departments concerned. (The Minister of Supply and Services may perform these services on behalf of departments.) Records are maintained of commitments made under contract that will fall due in succeeding years, since the Government must be prepared in future to ask Parliament for appropriations to cover them. Any unexpended amounts in the annual appropriations lapse at the end of the year for which they are granted, but for thirty days subsequent to March 31 payments may be made and charged to the previous year's appropriations for debts payable prior to the end of that fiscal year.

Under the Financial Administration Act, every payment pursuant to an appropriation is made under the control and direction of the Receiver General by cheque or other instrument in such form and authenticated in such manner as the Treasury Board may direct. In practice, such cheques or instruments are cleared daily by the chartered banks through the Bank of Canada to the Cheque Adjustment Division of the Receiver General's office, and reimbursement is made by means of a cheque drawn on the Receiver General's account with the Bank of Canada.

## Public Debt

In addition to the collection and disbursement of public money for budgetary and non-budgetary purposes, the Government receives and disburses substantial sums in connection with its public debt operations. The Minister of Finance is authorized to borrow money by the issue and sale of securities at such rate of interest and subject to such terms and conditions as the Governor in Council may approve. Although the specific authority of Parliament is required for new borrowings, the Financial Administration Act authorizes the Governor in Council to approve the borrowing of such sums of money as are required for the redemption of maturing or called securities and to ensure that the Consolidated Revenue Fund will be sufficient to meet lawfully authorized disbursements, he may also approve the temporary borrowing of such sums as are necessary for periods not exceeding six months. The Bank of Canada acts as the fiscal agent of the Government in the management of the public debt.

## Accounts and Financial Statements

Under the Financial Administration Act and subject to regulations of the Treasury Board, the Receiver General requires accounts to be kept to show the revenues of Canada, the expenditures made under each appropriation, other payments into and out of the Consolidated Revenue Fund, and such of the assets and direct and contingent liabilities as the Minister of Finance believes are required to give a true and fair view of the financial position of Canada. The statement of assets and liabilities is designed to disclose the amount of the net debt, which is determined by offsetting against the gross liabilities only those assets regarded currently as readily realizable or interest or revenue-producing. Fixed capital assets, such as government buildings and public works, are charged to budgetary expenditures at the time of acquisition or construction and are shown on the statement of assets and liabilities at a nominal value of $1.

Annually, on or before December 31 or, if Parliament is not then sitting, within any of the first fifteen days next thereafter that Parliament is sitting, the Public Accounts, prepared by the Receiver General, are laid before the House of Commons by the Minister of Finance. The Public Accounts contain a survey of the financial transactions of the fiscal year ended the previous March 31, statements of the revenues and expenditures for that year and of the assets and direct and contingent liabilities as at the end of that year, together with such other accounts and information as are necessary to show the financial transactions and financial position of Canada or which are required by law to be reported in the Public Accounts. Monthly financial statements are also published in the *Canada Gazette*.

## The Auditor General

The Government's accounts are subject to an independent examination by the Auditor General who is an officer of Parliament. With respect to expenditures, this examination is a post-audit for the purposes of reporting whether the accounts have been faithfully and properly kept, whether the money has been expended for the purposes for which it was appropriated by Parliament and whether the expenditures have been made as authorized. With respect to revenues, the Auditor General is required to ascertain that all public money is fully accounted for and that the rules and procedures applied are sufficient to ensure an effective check on the assessment, collection and proper allocation of the revenue. With respect to public property, he is required to satisfy himself that essential records are maintained and that the rules and procedures applied are sufficient to safeguard and control such property. The Auditor General reports to Parliament the results of his examination, calling attention to any case which he considers should be brought to the notice of the House. He also reports to Ministers, the Treasury Board or the Government any matter which in his opinion calls for attention so that remedial action may be taken promptly.

## Public Accounts Committee

It is the usual practice to refer the Public Accounts and the Auditor General's Report to the Public Accounts Committee of the House of Commons, which may review them and report its findings and recommendations to the House of Commons.

# Part Two

*READINGS*

*Organization*

Ashley, C. A., *The First Twenty-Five Years: A Study of Trans-Canada Air Lines.* Toronto, The Macmillan Company of Canada, Limited, 1963.

Ashley, C. A. and Smails, R. G. H., *Canadian Crown Corporations.* Toronto, The Macmillan Company of Canada, Limited, 1965.

Bowland, J. G., "Geographical Decentralization in the Canadian Federal Public Service." *Canadian Public Administration*, Vol. 10, No. 3 (September, 1967), pp. 323-61.

Bridges, The Right Hon. Lord, "Les Rapports entre le Gouvernement et les Sociétés de l'Etat." *Canadian Public Administration*, Vol. 7, No. 3 (September, 1964), pp. 309-23.

Bridges, The Right Hon. Lord, "The Relationships between Governments and Government-Controlled Corporations." *Canadian Public Administration*, Vol. 7, No. 3 (September, 1964), pp. 295-308.

Burns, R. M., "Co-operation in Government." *Canadian Tax Journal*, Vol. 7 (January-February, 1959), pp. 5-15.

Burns, R. M., "The Machinery of Federal-Provincial Relations: ii." *Canadian Public Administration*, Vol. 8, No. 4 (December, 1965), pp. 527-34.

Caldwell, G. H., "Unity of Command: A Comparison of the Top Level Organization Structures of the Government of Canada and of Large Scale Private Enterprises." *Canadian Public Administration*, Vol. 7, No. 4 (December, 1964), pp. 510-45.

Canada, Civil Service Commission, *The Analysis of Organization in the Government of Canada.* Ottawa, Queen's Printer, 1966.

Canada, *Royal Commission on Bilingualism and Biculturalism, Report,* Vol. 1. Ottawa, Queen's Printer, 1967.

Canada, *Royal Commission on Government Organization* (Glassco Commission) *Report:* Vol. 1, *Management of the Public Service*, reports 1-4; Vol. 2, *Supporting Services for Government*, reports 5-11; Vol. 3, *Supporting Services for Government*, reports 12-13 and *Services for the Public*, reports 14-18; Vol. 4, *Special Areas of Administration*, reports 19-23; Vol. 5, *The Organization of the Government of Canada*. Ottawa, Queen's Printer, 1962-1963.

Carr, D. W., "The Legislative-Administrative Structure in Canada: its Significance for Agricultural Resource Development." *Canadian Public Administration*, Vol. 5, No. 2 (June, 1962), pp. 156-71.

Carter, F. A. G. and Phillips, R. A. J., "Organizing for Northern Administration: a Practical Problem in Decentralization." *Canadian Public Administration*, Vol. 5, No. 1 (March, 1962), pp. 104-16.

Cole, Taylor, *The Canadian Bureaucracy and Federalism 1947-1965.* Denver, Colorado, University of Denver Press, 1966.

Corbett, D. C., *Politics and the Airlines.* Toronto, University of Toronto Press, 1965.

Côté, E. A., "The Public Services in a Bicultural Society." *Canadian Public Administration*, Vol. 11, No. 3 (Fall, 1968), pp. 280-90.

Des Roches, J. M., "The Evolution of the Organization of the Federal Government in Canada." *Canadian Public Administration*, Vol. 5, No. 4 (December, 1962), pp. 408-27.

Friedman, W., ed., *The Public Corporation: a Comparative Symposium*. Toronto, The Carswell Company, Limited, 1954.

Gallant, Edgar, "The Machinery of Federal-Provincial Relations: I." *Canadian Public Administration*, Vol. 8, No. 4 (December, 1965), pp. 515-26.

Gelinas, André, "Trois modes d'approche à la détermination de l'opportunité de la décentralisation de l'organisation politique principalement en système fédéral." *Canadian Public Administration*, Vol. 9, No. 1 (March, 1966), pp. 1-26.

Heeney, A. D. P., "Mackenzie King and the Cabinet Secretariat." *Canadian Public Administration*, Vol. 10, No. 3 (September, 1967), pp. 366-75.

Hodgetts, J. E., "The Grand Inquest on the Canadian Public Service." *Public Administration* (Australia), Vol. 22, No. 3 (September, 1963), pp. 226-41.

Hodgetts, J. E., "Should Canada be De-Commissioned? A Commoner's View of Royal Commissions." *Queen's Quarterly*, Vol. 70 (Winter, 1964), pp. 475-90.

Kristjanson, Kris, "Crown Corporations: Administrative Responsibility and Public Accountability." *Canadian Public Administration*, Vol. 11, No. 4 (Winter, 1968), pp. 454-59.

Kwavnick, D., "French Canadians and the Civil Service of Canada." *Canadian Public Administration*, Vol. 11, No. 1 (Spring, 1968), pp. 97-112.

Lyngseth, D. M., "The Use of Organization and Methods in Canadian Government." *Canadian Public Administration*, Vol. 5, No. 4 (December, 1962), pp. 428-92.

McDonald, G. P. A., "Labour, Manpower, and Government Reorganization." *Canadian Public Administration*, Vol. 10, No. 4 (December, 1967), pp. 471-98.

McLeod, T. H., "Glassco Commission Report." *Canadian Public Administration*, Vol. 6, No. 4 (December, 1963), pp. 386-406.

Musolf, L. D., "Canadian Public Enterprise: a Character Study." *American Political Science Review*, Vol. 50, No. 2 (June, 1956), pp. 405-21.

Plumptre, A. F. W., "Regionalism and the Public Service." *Canadian Public Administration*, Vol. 8, No. 4 (December, 1965), pp. 548-57.

Ritchie, R. S., et al., "The Glassco Commission Report." *Canadian Public Administration*, Vol. 5, No. 4 (December, 1962), pp. 385-401.

Rocher, G., "Bureaucracy and Welfare." *Canadian Welfare*, Vol. 39 (March-April, 1963), pp. 55-60.

Schindeler, Fred, "The Organization and Functions of the Executive Branch of Government in Ontario." *Canadian Public Administration*, Vol. 9, No. 4 (December, 1966), pp. 409-48.

Smiley, Donald V., "Public Administration and Canadian Federalism." *Canadian Public Administration*, Vol. 7, No. 3 (September, 1964), pp. 371-88.

Taylor, K. W., "Co-ordination in Administration." *Proceedings of the Ninth Annual Conference*, Toronto, Institute of Public Administration of Canada, 1957, pp. 253-73.

Tunnoch, G. V., "The Glassco Commission: Did It Cost More Than It Was Worth?" *Canadian Public Administration*, Vol. 7, No. 3 (September, 1964), pp. 389-97.

Yeomans, D. R., "Decentralization of Authority." *Canadian Public Administration*, Vol. 12, No. 1 (Spring, 1969), pp. 9-25.

## Personnel

Best, J. C., "Management and Staff Relations in the Public Service." *Canadian Public Administration*, Vol. 4, No. 2 (June, 1961), pp. 168-76.

Blackburn, G. A., "A Bilingual and Bicultural Public Service." *Canadian Public Administration*, Vol. 12, No. 1 (Spring, 1969), pp. 36-44.

Brady, A., "Training and Development of Public Administrators." *University of Toronto Quarterly*, Vol. 22 (April, 1953), pp. 217-29.

Callard, K. B., *Advanced Administrative Training in the Public Service*. Toronto, University of Toronto Press, 1958.

Canada, Civil Service Commission, *Personnel Administration in the Civil Service: a Review of Civil Service Legislation*. Ottawa, Queen's Printer, 1958.

Canada, Civil Service Commission, *Report of the Preparatory Committee on Collective Bargaining*. Ottawa, Queen's Printer, 1965.

Canada, Department of Labour, "The Public Service Staff Relations Act", in A. M. Willms and W. D. K. Kernaghan, eds., *Public Administration in Canada*. (Toronto, Methuen Publications, 1968), pp. 391-98.

Canada, National Joint Council of the Public Service, *The National Joint Council of the Public Service of Canada, 1944-1964*. Ottawa, Queen's Printer, 1964.

Canada, *Royal Commission on Administrative Classification in the Public Service, Report*. Ottawa, King's Printer, 1946.

Dowdell, R. H., "Personnel Administration in the Federal Public Service," in A. M. Willms and W. D. K. Kernaghan, eds., *Public Administration in Canada*. Toronto, Methuen Publications, 1968), pp. 360-88.

Dymond, W. R., "The Role of the Union in the Public Service as Opposed to its Role in Private Business." *Proceedings of the Fifth Annual Conference*. Toronto, Institute of Public Administration of Canada, 1953, pp. 55-64.

Frankel, S. J., *A Model for Negotiation and Arbitration between the Canadian Government and its Civil Servants*. Montreal, McGill University Press, 1962.

Frankel, S. J., *Staff Relations in the Civil Service: the Canadian Experience*. Montreal, McGill University Press, 1962.

Gosselin, E., et al., "L'administration publique dans un pays bilingue et biculturel: actualités et propos." *Canadian Public Administration*, Vol. 6, No. 4 (December, 1963), pp. 407-33.

Gow, J. I., "La Nouvelle Loi de la Fonction publique dans la province de Québec." *Canadian Public Administration*, Vol. 9, No. 1 (March, 1966), pp. 96-107.

Mankiewicz, R. H., "Sur le droit de grève dans les services publics au Canada." *Relations Industrielles*, Vol. 11 (September, 1956), pp. 254-67.

Morgan, J. S., "Staffing the Public Welfare Services." *Canadian Public Administration*, Vol. 3, No. 2 (June, 1960), pp. 157-70.

Porter, J., "The Bureaucratic Elite: a Reply to Professor Rowat." *Canadian Journal of Economics and Political Science*, Vol. 25, No. 2 (May, 1959), pp. 205-7.

Porter, J., "Higher Public Servants and the Bureaucratic Elite in Canada." *Canadian Journal of Economics and Political Science*, Vol. 24, No. 4 (November, 1958), pp. 483-501.

Prives, M. Z., "Career and Promotion in the Federal Civil Service of Canada." *Canadian Public Administration*, Vol. 3, No. 2 (June, 1960), pp. 179-90.

Robertson, R. G., "The Canadian Parliament and Cabinet in the Face of Modern Demands." *Canadian Public Administration*, Vol. 11, No. 3 (Fall, 1968), pp. 272-79.

Rowat, Donald C., "On John Porter's Bureaucratic Elite in Canada." *Canadian Journal of Economics and Political Science*, Vol. 25, No. 2 (May, 1959), pp. 205-7.

Vaison, Robert A., "Collective Bargaining in the Federal Public Service: the Achievement of a Milestone in Personnel Relations." *Canadian Public Administration*, Vol. 12, No. 1 (Spring, 1969), pp. 108-22.

*Finance*

Balls, H. R., "The Budget and its Function." *Cost and Management*, Vol. 41 (October, 1967), pp. 25-28.

Balls, H. R., "The Budget and the National Accounts." *Cost and Management*, Vol. 41 (November, 1967), pp. 28-31.

Balls, H. R., "Issue Control and Pre-Audit for Authority: the Functions of the Comptroller of the Treasury." *Canadian Public Administration*, Vol. 3, No. 2 (June, 1960), pp. 118-33.

Balls, H. R., "The Public Accounts, their Purposes and Factors Affecting their Form: an Administrative View." *Canadian Public Administration*, Vol. 7, No. 4 (December, 1964), pp. 422-41.

Balls, H. R., "The Public Accounts Committee." *Canadian Public Administration*, Vol. 6, No. 1 (March, 1963), pp. 15-28.

Benson, E. J., "Budget Breakthrough: Adoption of PPB." *Canadian Tax Journal*, Vol. 16, No. 3 (May-June, 1968), pp. 161-67.

Canada, *Report of the Auditor General*. Ottawa, Queen's Printer, annual.

Currie, G. N., "Efficiency vs. Service in Public Administration." *Canadian Public Administration*, Vol. 7, No. 2 (June, 1964), pp. 165-74.

Fowke, Donald V., "PPB for Provinces." *Canadian Public Administration*, Vol. 12, No. 1 (Spring, 1969), pp. 72-77.

Franks, C. E. S., "The Saskatchewan Public Accounts Committee." *Canadian Public Administration*, Vol. 9, No. 3 (September, 1966), pp. 348-66.

Henderson, A. M., "Treasury Board, the Comptroller of the Treasury, the Auditor General." *Canadian Tax Journal*, Vol. 8, No. 6 (November-December, 1960), pp. 412-14.

Huson, A. G., "Business and Public Administration." *Business Quarterly*, Vol. 22 (Winter, 1957), pp. 389-97.

Johnson, A. W. "Efficiency in Government and Business." *Canadian Public Administration*, Vol. 6, No. 3 (September, 1963), pp. 245-60.

Johnson, A. W., "Planning and Budgeting." *Canadian Public Administration*, Vol. 2, No. 3 (September, 1959), pp. 145-53.

Kristjanson, Baldur H., "Some Thoughts on Planning at the Federal Level." *Canadian Public Administration*, Vol. 8, No. 2 (June, 1965), pp. 143-51.

Little, P. L. and Mitchell, C. L., "The Program Budget: Planning and Control for the Public Sector." *Cost and Management*, Vol. 41 (September, 1967), pp. 22-26.

MacLean, R. D., "An Examination of the Role of the Comptroller of the Treasury." *Canadian Public Administration*, Vol. 7, No. 1 (March, 1964), pp. 1-133.

Parizeau, Jacques, "The Five-Year Budget." *Canadian Public Administration*, Vol. 9, No. 2 (June, 1966), pp. 201-10.

Sterns, A. A., "Implementing the Glassco Report." *Cost and Management*, Vol. 42 (January, 1968), pp. 25-30.

Sterns, A. A., "The Prelude to Action on the Glassco Report." *Cost and Management*, Vol. 41 (December, 1967), pp. 20-23.

Sterns, A. A., "The Functions of the Treasury Board," in A. M. Willms and W. D. K. Kernaghan, eds., *Public Administration in Canada*. Toronto, Methuen Publications, 1968.

Stevenson, I., "The Auditor-General: Financial Watchdog of Parliament." *Canadian Chartered Accountant*, Vol. 69 (November, 1956), pp. 399-403.

Ward, N., "The Committee on Estimates." *Canadian Public Administration*, Vol. 6, No. 1 (March, 1963), pp. 35-42.

Ward, N., *The Public Purse: a study in Canadian Democracy*. Toronto, University of Toronto Press, 1962.

White, W. L. and Strick, J. C., "The Treasury Board and Parliament." *Canadian Public Administration*, Vol. 10, No. 2 (June, 1967), pp. 209-22.

Young, John H., "Planning in Canada: Problems and Prospects." *Canadian Public Administration*, Vol. 8, No. 2 (June, 1965), pp. 146-52.

# PART THREE

# Politics and Administration

Before 1945, most scholars and practitioners of public administration viewed the separation of politics and policy from administration as the existing and desirable method of conducting government business. The functions of public servants were ostensibly limited to the implementation of policy decisions taken by elected representatives of the people.

In the immediate post-war period, a number of political scientists launched a successful assault on the validity of this traditional politics-administration dichotomy. The involvement of public servants in the policy-making process and in the exercise of discretionary powers was clearly recognized and documented. Moreover, the extensive inter-action of public officials with legislatures, courts, pressure groups, the mass media, and the general public manifested the prominent position of the bureaucracy in the political system.

In this part, the first of the selections demonstrating this intimate link between politics and administration is John Porter's analysis of the status of the bureaucracy in Canada's power structure. Mitchell Sharp, a former member of the bureaucratic elite, reminisces about the participation of senior public servants in policy formation and in politics. James Eayrs describes this participation with particular reference to the realm of Canadian Foreign Policy. By examining the related issue of the political activity of public servants, I raise the question of reconciling bureaucratic neutrality with political rights.

The three subsequent articles centre on the mechanics and influence of pressure-group activity in the administrative sphere. Helen Jones Dawson and Bruce Doern focus on the operations of particular pressure groups in the administrative process, whereas Robert Armstrong demonstrates the bureaucracy's success in exerting pressure on policy making through its employee organizations.

Then, Maurice Lamontagne challenges those who point to the enormous influence of the bureaucracy on policy determination. He contends that "the twilight of civil servants" is at hand and that new and competing power centres are developing in the Canadian political system. Bruce Doern argues for more non-governmental involvement in the policy process but is especially critical of Royal Commissions as the primary means to achieve this end.

# 10 Power and the Canadian Bureaucratic Elite*

## John Porter

The sheer growth of governmental operations over the last half-century has created within civil services and administrative agencies a new and relatively autonomous system of power and decision-making. In part this autonomy arises from the specialized function of public services as the administrative arms of governments, but also because of the development of a distinct career system and professional norms which are quite different from those in other institutions. Thus the significant thing to look for in examining governmental bureaucracy is the extent to which these specific qualities making for autonomy have developed. Particularly important in this context are the careers of those within Canada's federal bureaucracy. Whether bureaucracy draws its ability from all social classes or only from the educated classes, it constitutes a formidable structure of power based on knowledge. Thus governmental bureaucracy occupies a strategic place in the over-all structure of power, particularly in relation to the political system.

The question of whether civil servants have more power than ministers cannot be answered without examining the interpersonal relations that develop in particular cases. Such examinations are usually beyond the reach of the social investigator. However, some general picture of this power relationship can be gathered by examining the social background

---

* John Porter, *The Vertical Mosaic* (Toronto, University of Toronto Press, 1965), pp. 417-56 (reprinted and abridged by permission of author and publisher).

and training of both senior civil servants and politicians. Where career data suggest that senior civil servants are experts, both in a technical discipline and in the administration of a particular department, and that politicians are predominantly amateurs, it can be surmised that bureaucratic power has the capacity to challenge political power.

It is possible to separate those characteristics which maximize power for governmental bureaucracy. Where a bureaucracy is fully rationalized and where it has a monopoly of experts, the conditions are present for optimum power. Under these circumstances political parties, in government or in opposition, have a minimum of independent experts. Moreover, because it is fully rationalized as a career system the bureaucracy has maximized efficiency.

Along with rationalization we can consider another continuum which measures the degree of rivalry which exists between a bureaucracy and other parts of the social structure for experts. The more a society concentrates its experts in governmental bureaucracy, the less external criticism of policy is possible. Under these circumstances we can say that the bureaucracy is unrivalled. Factors which determine a bureaucracy's location on this rivalled-unrivalled continuum are the existence of strong and competent party bureaucracies staffed with experts to provide amateur politicians with briefs through which party objectives, if there are any, can be achieved. A further factor is the existence of strong criticism outside the bureaucracy, which means considerable separation of the bureaucracy and the institutions of higher learning which are the most important alternative sources of experts.

In their search for technical competence bureaucracies break down traditional class barriers. Thus a fully rationalized bureaucracy is an open one as far as class recruitment is concerned. By examining the social origins of higher officials it should be possible to determine the extent to which a bureaucracy is open or closed. There is then a third continuum on which any existing bureaucracy can be placed, that is, the continuum between the poles of being completely closed or completely open in terms of the social class or group from which recruits are drawn.

Within any one bureaucracy the characteristics of *rationality, rivalry,* and *openness* can be found in various combinations. The bureaucracy which is ideal from the point of view of efficiency, minimization of power, and social mobility opportunities is that which is *rationalized, rivalled,* and *open.* The type which comes closest to Weber's fully developed bureaucracy is that which is *rationalized, unrivalled,* and *open.* It is the absence of rivalry which enables the bureaucracy to assert its influence over political chiefs. The need to recruit ability from the widest social base has the effect of "levelling" social classes. Ethnic bars, religious tests, and recruiting systems based on class privileges would be irrationalities. A system which is *rationalized, unrivalled,* and *closed* carries the development of bureaucratic power one stage further for under these conditions there is an efficient bureaucratic machine which has a monopoly of experts drawn from a narrow section of the social structure with possibly a considerable degree of occupational inheritance.

This typology of bureaucracy attempts to provide a framework with which to analyze bureaucratic power in the social system. It is a way of looking at some of the data of bureaucracy in terms of the prevailing values of the society. It is not sufficient to see civil services simply as extensions of the executive branches of government. Rather they have an organic relationship to the rest of the society. Given the general trend of western values, a bureaucracy which is efficient, provides a career open to the talented, and does not monopolize talent or usurp power can be said to be functioning adequately. Whether or not bureaucracy is functioning adequately in terms of social values cannot be dealt with entirely by a study of the careers of senior civil servants. However, through a study of recruitment, the bureaucratic career, the organization of specialists, political influences in appointments, and so forth, some general trends should be discerned which in turn may indicate further areas of investigation.

## Social Background and Careers

We shall now examine career and social background data of the federal bureaucratic elite as it existed in 1953. Later, we shall look at what happened to the senior bureaucracy after the Liberal defeat of 1957, that is, during the Diefenbaker administration. The bureaucratic elite for this study is composed of 243 senior officials of the federal government departments, agencies, and Crown corporations. Fairly uniform data were obtained for 202 (or 83 per cent) of the 243 people. The analysis which follows is of the 202 people divided into three levels: deputy minister (40 people); associate/assistant deputy minister (77 people); and "director" (56 people). There is also a group of Crown corporation executives (29 people).

## *Education*

One frequently voiced criticism of the Canadian public service has been its inability to attract men of high calibre into its senior and intermediate grades. Although there may be some element of truth in this notion, the upper levels constitute what is probably the most highly trained group of people to be found anywhere in Canada. It is not so much the inability to attract men of high calibre as the inability to attract them when young, and to get them to devote their careers to the public service.

Of the bureaucratic elite of 202 persons, 159 (78.7 per cent) had university degrees. In the deputy minister category 35 of the 40 persons (87.5 per cent) were graduates; in the associate/assistant deputy category, 57 out of 77 (74 per cent); in the director category, 44 out of 56 (78.6 per cent); and in the Crown corporation group, 23 out of 29 (79 per cent).

A further indication of the intellectual quality of the bureaucratic elite was that almost one-fifth (18.3 per cent) had taught in a university at some stage in their careers, usually early. A fair number of this group of former university teachers came to the bureaucracy from the higher professorial ranks, and had distinguished themselves as academics before becoming public servants.

Some speculative remarks might be ventured about this intellectualizing of the upper levels of the bureaucracy. According to one observer the civil service in Canada has employed almost all the experts in many fields.[1] It must be added that there is scarcely a scientific discipline, social or natural, to which some public servant has not made an important contribution. Many government departments maintain large research branches which are designed primarily to service the bureaucracy in its role of advising politicians, but which incidentally give the bureaucracy that power which rests on knowledge. These research activities reach beyond the civil service in two ways. Many departments make grants to universities or members of university staffs to investigate problems in which the bureaucracy has some interest. Secondly, many academics are hired as consultants or become temporary government employees while they investigate particular problems.

The high formal qualifications of senior bureaucrats, as well as the close ties with university life through the ex-professor and the research organization, tend to take the Canadian bureaucracy towards the unrivalled end of the rivalled-unrivalled continuum. It is the bureaucracy which has that power which stems from insight into the practicability of policy. The monopolizing of experts could be reduced if there were effective research organizations independent of government.

---

[1] Donald Eldon, "Toward a Well Informed Parliament," *Queen's Quarterly*, Vol. 64 (Winter, 1957). See also John J. Deutsch, "Parliament and the Civil Service," *Queen's Quarterly*, Vol. 64 (Winter, 1957). The latter says: "The federal government is by far the largest employer in the country of expert and trained personnel" (p. 568).

# Career Patterns

Equally striking from the point of view of the theory of bureaucracy was the absence of the fully developed bureaucratic career. This factor was measured in two ways. One method was by the proportion of their working lives that senior officials had spent in the public service. Only about one-half (52.9 per cent) of the 202 persons had spent more than half their working lives in the public service. About the same proportion was found for all the categories being considered.

The second way of measuring the development of the bureaucratic career was to determine how many of the elite were bureaucratic outsiders at the time of their appointments to senior positions. One-quarter (24.7 per cent) of these senior public servants were "jobbed in" from outside, the largest proportion (31 per cent) being with the Crown corporations, and the smallest proportion (21.4 per cent) at the "director" level which was also the level at which the largest proportion (30.4 per cent) had spent their entire careers in the service.

In discussing the problem of recruitment to the senior ranks of the public service, John Deutsch has said: "It is apparent that over the years the service has not produced its own leaders in adequate numbers. . . . Far too often the personnel required for senior positions is not found within the service and is obtained from outside."[2] It would seem that the Canadian service was far from that developed stage of the graduated career where the top posts came after a long series of promotions. As we have seen, this type of career applied to only 23.8 per cent of the bureaucratic elite.

It is the principle of neutrality rather than efficiency which is endangered by outside appointments at the higher levels. Although the proportion of transfers from political to bureaucratic roles was relatively small, and not out of Canadian tradition, there may have been other political considerations in bureaucratic appointments. Men of sufficient professional status to be appointed directly to high rank were not likely to be out of sympathy with the government which appointed them. It should be mentioned that 10 of the 21 political appointments were to departmental boards and commissions. There seems no reason why these posts should be earmarked as political rewards because in many cases they were also filled by career men. Most boards and commissions are sufficiently integrated into departmental structures that their top jobs could well be the career goals of a neutral bureaucracy. Perhaps the most difficult problem associated with appointments at a high level from

---

[2] John J. Deutsch, "Some Thoughts on the Public Service," *Canadian Journal of Economics and Political Science*, Vol. 23, No. 1 (February, 1957), p. 85.

outside the service is that of morale. It is unlikely that able people could be attracted to devote their careers to public service when the rewards at the top go to outsiders.

## Ethnic, Regional, and Religious Representation

Modern bureaucracies ideally require people who have been socially neutralized and who have divested themselves of interests in social groups and institutions involved in the struggle for power. Because the bases of power associations are frequently ethnic, regional, or religious the idea that these groups should be "represented" in the bureaucracy contradicts the notion of the official as the servant of the state. Ethnic, regional, and religious affiliations are not rational qualifications for office. Therefore, in the fully developed bureaucracy, and in its elite, one would expect to find these groups represented in about the same proportion as they are to be found in the general population if the following assumptions are met: that educational facilities to meet the qualifications are equal as between ethnic groups, regions, and religions; that no rights to offices are denied on ethnic, regional, or religious grounds; and that there is equal motivation in these groups to become public servants. Where higher offices are disproportionately distributed we do not know, without further investigation, which of these assumptions have not been met.

Canadian federalism has imposed ethnic, regional, and religious representation on many Canadian institutions. As one Canadian cabinet minister said in discussing French-Canadian representation in the higher bureaucracy, "there are two principles to be observed, the efficiency of the service and the promotion of national unity."[3] The goal of national unity can interfere with the efficiency of the service through recruitment and promotional practices which are not rationalized. In the theoretically ideal bureaucracy the candidate for office neither gains nor loses as a result of his ethnic, religious, or regional origins.

In view of the demands made at various times for greater French-Canadian representation in the civil service it is not surprising to find that they do not have a proportionate share of the top posts. Of the entire elite of 202, only 27 (13.4 per cent) were French Canadian although this group made up about one-third of the population. However, almost all these 27 were in the two top-rank categories of which they make up

---

[3] Ian Mackenzie, then Minister of Veterans Affairs, quoted by Frank Flaherty, "Why so few French Canadians in the Civil Service?" *Saturday Night* (July 19, 1947).

18.8 per cent. It must be remembered that French-Canadian education has not provided a large reservoir of administrators who could eventually be promoted to the higher levels. It is likely also that the motivation of French Canadians to serve the centralized state is not as great as it is with English Canadians, although the limited opportunities for French Canadians to move up hierarchies in the private corporate world should make the bureaucracy an attractive alternative. It would appear, then, that as far as higher posts are concerned the efficiency of the service has been as important as the promotion of national unity. Other ethnic groups in Canada, with the exception of Jews, are scarcely represented at all in the higher bureaucracy.

If the same assumptions which were made for ethnicity hold for regional origin, the higher bureaucracy should also be regionally "representative." Ontario, with 32.8 per cent of the 1951 population and 38.6 per cent of the elite, was the only region over-represented. The Atlantic provinces, Quebec, and British Columbia were under-represented. The Atlantic provinces which together had 11.5 per cent of the population had 8.9 per cent of the elite. Quebec's share of the population was 28.9 per cent, but it had only 21.3 per cent of the elite, while British Columbia with 8.3 per cent of the population had only 4.4 per cent of the elite. The prairie provinces which, taken together, had 18.2 per cent of the population came closer to a balanced representation with 16.8 per cent of the elite. Ten per cent of the elite were born outside Canada. The regions which were most under-represented had the greatest proportion of outside appointments. A little more than one-half of those from Quebec were outsiders while from Ontario only one-fifth were. Distance from the capital and intervening job opportunities probably account to some extent for the disproportionate representation of British Columbia. The under-representation of Quebec can be considered an ethnic and educational factor rather than a regional one.

Religious qualifications for office belong to the pre-rationalized bureaucracies. It is unlikely that religious affiliation is important for recruitment to the federal civil service at any level. Because the public servant should be content with "anonymity and obscurity" religion does not have the social function that it formerly had in economic roles, for example. None the less, the religious affiliations of the bureaucratic elite are interesting because of the two ways in which they differed from those of the economic elite. First, the nonconformist Protestant denominations replaced Anglicanism as the dominant faiths, and, secondly, the Roman Catholic church had a greater proportion of adherents in the bureaucratic than in the economic elite although it was still very much under-represented when compared to the Catholic proportion of the general population.

## Social Class Origins

Entrance to the Canadian bureaucratic elite depends on high educational qualifications. The fact that so much importance has been attached to these qualifications probably helps to account for the large number of outsiders recruited for high posts, and the little internal promotion from the lower categories to the higher. We have already noted that almost four out of five of the higher public servants graduated from university. In comparison, those who have university education make up a very small part of the total population. The demand of technical competence has narrowed the recruiting base to that fragment of the population who are willing and financially able to go to university.

Although the Canadian public service does not provide an avenue of upward mobility for the broad base of the social pyramid it is not at the same time an exclusive preserve of the upper classes. In this respect the bureaucratic elite differs considerably from the economic elite where about a third was recruited from elite families, and almost half came from families in the higher middle and upper classes. This tendency was much more marked for the top 100 corporation directors. The evidence that the recruiting base for the bureaucratic elite is lower in the class system than for the economic elite is varied. In the first place there was almost no internal recruitment – that is the passing on of jobs from father to son. A smaller proportion of the bureaucratic elite was from elite families and a smaller proportion attended private schools. A greater proportion were affiliated with the lower status, nonconformist denominations.

There has not, therefore, been a great deal of "levelling" of the social class system as a result of the growth of governmental bureaucracy in Canada. There never was, of course, "inherited avocational administration by notables" in Canada, at least not in the post-colonial period, so that any "levelling" process would have begun at a lower point. To some extent the reverse process has set in. The demands of efficiency and technical competence have meant that the bureaucracy has been drawing its top personnel mainly from the middle levels of the class system.

To draw some conclusions from these career and social background data it is necessary to return to the models of bureaucracy and society presented earlier, and to look at the Canadian bureaucracy in terms of the continuums of rationalized-non-rationalized, rivalled-unrivalled, open-closed. Factors drawing it away from the rationalized extreme are principally the absence of the bureaucratic career, but the tendency to recruit outsiders as representatives of particular interests and the remnants of political considerations in appointments are also important. Counteracting these tendencies are the high formal qualifications of the senior men. The quasi-monopoly of skills and knowledge in some important areas, the link with universities, and the absence of strong party or other research organizations would bring the Canadian bureaucracy towards the unrivalled end of the rivalled-unrivalled continuum. The social class and ethnic origins would suggest that the bureaucracy is more closed than open.

If the Canadian bureaucracy is to be brought closer to the ideal of rationalized, rivalled, and open it would be necessary to develop more fully the bureaucratic career, particularly by reducing the number of outside appointments at high levels, so that these senior positions become the career goals that they should be to conform to the model. It is also important that the skills and knowledge of the highly trained be distributed through other institutional structures so that criticism and alternative policies can be built on firmer ground. Policies of recruitment and promotion must seek the ability that lies at the lower levels of the bureaucratic hierarchy and the class system.

Something should be said about the social homogeneity of the bureaucratic elite, for it is similarity of social type which makes an elite a cohesive group distinct from those at the top of other institutional hierarchies. Homogeneity results from common socialization processes and from common interaction. These senior public servants have, by and large, a common background in the social class and educational systems of Canada. Their high level of education and their link with the universities would suggest commonly held intellectual values. It is likely also that the recruitment of outsiders tends to select those who have similar views about the role of government in national development. There are many areas of formal and informal interaction common to, and at times exclusive to, the bureaucratic elite. For one thing they live in a relatively small and occupationally homogeneous city. In their formal roles they come together in a large number of inter-departmental committees and conferences at home and abroad. Informally they meet in a variety of contexts. Moreover, the higher bureaucracy has some cohesiveness as a group and an orientation to intellectual values, particularly among those concerned with economic and social policy.

# 1957 and after

The 1957 federal election broke up the close relationship which had lasted more than two decades between the higher bureaucracy and

Liberal administrations. In many respects the two groups were each other's creatures. The bureaucracy had become both larger and more efficient as Liberal longevity increased.

The avocational character of Canadian politics meant that while cabinet ministers came and went senior officials stayed on and provided continuity. The recruitment of the bureaucratic outsider suggested at least some sympathy with the political party in office. The tendency for the higher bureaucratic posts to become linked to politics with entrance to the cabinet, as in the case of Mr. Pearson and Mr. Pickersgill, and the drift towards monopolizing of experts within the bureaucracy meant that the Liberal party never had to build up its own party research facilities. It has been pointed out by John Meisel that civil servants rather than party experts or officials were the main creators of the Liberal party programme in the 1957 general election.[4] There had been, too, in the appointments to those periphery agencies and boards some political patronage or, if not that, ties of personal loyalty to C. D. Howe. This close partnership of bureaucrats and Liberals worked harmoniously with foreign and native corporate elites during one of the most prosperous periods in Canada's economic history.

Election night in June 1957 came as a shock to many senior officials in Ottawa. They faced a strange political environment in which now they were to serve those who in the House of Commons had been the critics of their defeated masters, and so indirectly critics of themselves. They had seen a succession of relatively ineffective opposition leaders come and go. John Diefenbaker, the new prime minister, scarcely fitted in with the recent traditions of Canadian politics. Moreover, he had ideas about increasing trade with the United Kingdom, stemming the foreign takeover of Canadian corporations, building the South Saskatchewan Dam, and other things which the bureaucracy viewed with some scepticism.

After six years of Conservative government the questions could in part be answered. The bureaucracy remained intact, although it is unlikely that it ever achieved the close working relationship with Conservative ministers that it had enjoyed over a long period of time with the Liberals. Moreover, there was no effort on the part of the Conservative ministry to break up the bureaucracy, either by forcing retirements or by appointing outsiders known to be their political supporters. The bureaucracy persisted because it is indispensable and does have something of an autonomous role in the structure of power. That there was

---

4 John Meisel, "The Formulation of Liberal and Conservative Programmes in the 1957 Canadian General Election," *Canadian Journal of Economics and Political Science,* Vol. 26, No. 4 (November, 1960), pp. 565-74.

no flight of senior officials suggests that in spite of the close relationship between Liberals and bureaucrats there had developed, independent of that relationship, some professional norms of public service.

There were, of course, the early pulling out and pressuring out of a few, and some failures to reappoint those whose terms had expired. Although there is little doubt that in some cases there was serious disagreement with government policy which left no alternative but resignation for senior officials, some of the resignations would have come anyway and some were close enough to, or over, retirement age that conflict between officials and politicians could have played only a minor part. These resignations were not sufficient in number, nor were they from crucial posts, to change significantly the character of the senior bureaucracy.

It is evident that the movement out of the public service at the higher levels was at no greater rate during the Conservative period than it was during the Liberal period. Moreover, it would seem, because about one-third of those who left went to employment elsewhere rather than retirement, that there is an incomplete development of the bureaucratic career, but this seems to have nothing to do with the political party in office. The structure of the public service, at least as measured by the type of appointment to the top rank, or as judged by the trickle out from the top, was no different under Conservatives than it was under Liberals.

We have not examined the movement out, or the new appointments into, elite positions below the deputy minister level, or of the senior executives of the Crown corporations. In every department almost all those who were appointed to the assistant and associate deputy minister rank came from inside the service. There is no evidence that the movement out of the public service at this level was any greater under the Conservative government than it was under the Liberals. Thus it would seem that the federal bureaucracy is gradually reaching a stage of being fully developed where it recruits its senior officers from within. Inasmuch as this trend continues, with no greater loss from the top, it might be concluded that the federal bureaucracy has acquired a position of relative autonomy within the over-all structure of power. This stability is particularly marked in the departments of Finance and External Affairs. It would seem, then, that even where government policy is little more than one of stabilizing the economy that the problems involved and the need for continuity in administration ensure the bureaucracy of a particular role in the power processes.

# 11 The Bureaucratic Elite and Policy Formation*

## Mitchell Sharp

What I wish to convey to you are personal impressions of what it is like to be a senior civil servant and comments on the role of civil servants in the formulation of policy in Canada.

First, contrary to what I had expected and contrary to the common opinion, I found a civil service career to be far from dull and humdrum. Those 16 years were full of stimulating experiences and highly exciting activities. Like so many others, I was called to Ottawa early in the war to do a wartime job in the Department of Finance. But when the time came to return to private business, I made the choice to remain in Ottawa and I have never regretted it.

The main reason for that decision was one man – the late Clifford Clark, Deputy Minister of Finance. The contribution of this man to the Canadian nation will never be fully appreciated, because the story can never be fully told of his influence upon the course of events. Being a civil servant, he worked anonymously, in the background, his views and his actions finding their expression in official utterances of Ministers and in the statutes approved by Parliament. Nor would he have wished it

* Mitchell Sharp, "Reflections of a Former Civil Servant," (reprinted by permission of author from notes used in an informal talk to a group of Toronto businessmen, November 14, 1958, and reproduced by the Civil Service Commission, Ottawa). The author, now Secretary of State for External Affairs, was formerly Deputy Minister of the Department of Trade and Commerce.

otherwise and he inculcated into all of us his ideal of the good civil servant.

To a greater degree than at any time before or since, the Department of Finance, during Dr. Clark's tenure as Deputy Minister, was the central idea-generating department of government. Under any circumstances, the Treasury, through control of the purse strings, has a key position in the Ottawa hierarchy. But Dr. Clark was not content that the Treasury should merely control. His curiosity and his energy found expression in the advocacy of policies touching every aspect of Canada's economic life. Price control, housing, family allowances, veterans' benefits, export credits insurance, and agricultural price supports are only a few subjects of the many, apart from those of a purely financial character, on which he had imaginative views – and to which he made significant contributions.

I was fortunate, too, in working under three excellent Ministers. The first was J. L. Ilsley. He is a man of great intelligence and broad human understanding. If he had a fault as a Minister, it was his over-conscientiousness. He spent hours debating difficult problems. And after he had made his decision, he spent hours debating whether he had made the right decision. It was strenuous to work under him but at least one had the satisfaction of knowing that the opposition was not likely to succeed in raising an argument he had not thoroughly considered. One of the most important jobs of a senior civil servant is guessing what questions or arguments the Opposition is likely to raise in Parliament and providing the answers in advance.

D. C. Abbott was a different kind of Minister. He had the characteristics of the good corporation lawyer, one of which is to be able to master a brief in short order. His mind was extraordinarily quick. It was a pleasure to sit before him on the floor of the Commons when the House was in Committee. It required only two or three whispered words of advice for him to get to his feet and in reply to a question give an answer lasting 5 minutes. It seemed to me that of the Ministers I had the privilege to know, he understood best the political art of the possible. On occasion he could show remarkable courage, but he selected the issues on which to fight with great care and a sure instinct.

C. D. Howe, of course, was unique. It is most improbable that we shall see his like in Canadian politics in our time. His intuition on economic matters was little short of miraculous and his fund of knowledge the despair of his advisers. I tried my best, when his Deputy, to keep myself well-informed about economic developments in Canada. Yet I can say truthfully that seldom was I able to tell Mr. Howe anything about which he had not already heard or surmised. His wide acquaintanceship was one of the reasons. He knew every important business man in Canada and they seemed to have made a practice of talking to "C.D." whether they wanted anything from the government or not. Most of all, they seemed to want his opinion.

Interplay of personalities and the constant exchange of views among the leading public servants that formed such a characteristic and stimulating feature of the Ottawa scene when I was there also explain why I got so much satisfaction out of working in Ottawa.

Some observers have referred disparagingly to the Ottawa "brains trust". Those who use this term, of course, do not think that those who are supposed to comprise this mythical body either have brains or can be trusted. Needless to say, there is no "brains trust" that pretends to know all the answers and there never has been. Indeed, on many matters it was considered undesirable to try to reach common views for presentation to Ministers. To have attempted to do so might have given a quite unjustified authority to the resulting piece of paper or have glossed over differences of interpretation that Ministers should have been aware of.

Fortunately, however, the leading advisers of the Government do not work in water-tight compartments within their Departments jealously guarding their prerogatives; they make a practice of consultation. They do this partly in formally constituted committees created by Cabinet and partly, and even more importantly, in informal gatherings at lunch, at dinner, at receptions, at evening parties and at the fishing club. It is taken for granted at most Ottawa social gatherings that the wives gravitate to one end of the room while their husbands collect at the other for that infinitely fascinating occupation of "talking shop".

From observation and from conversation with civil servants in other countries, I have come to the conclusion that this close contact and constant exchange of views among leading civil servants in Ottawa is in many respects unique. In Washington inter-departmental consultation hardly exists except in formally constituted committees. In London, there is greater informality during working hours than in Washington, but after hours civil servants depart for their homes in widely separated suburbs of the city and have relatively few social contacts.

It was therefore something of an intellectual adventure to be a senior public servant in Ottawa during my time and I am sure it continues to be so. One's horizon was always being broadened by contact with a variety of first class minds working on a variety of matters of national interest. And I might add, one's pet ideas had to be supported by more than mere enthusiasm to survive the abundant doses of cold water that were politely poured on them by fellow civil servants. I can assure you that it is much more difficult to be an acknowledged authority on fiscal and monetary policy, foreign affairs, full employment, trade and like matters in the civil service community of Ottawa than it is in the business community of Toronto.

From time to time someone refers disparagingly to "ivory tower" thinking in Ottawa. I suppose there is always some of that kind of thinking everywhere, including Ottawa, and I, for one, believe that it has its place. To suggest, however, that the thinking that goes on behind the scenes in Ottawa is highly theoretical and divorced from the everyday world, is to misjudge the intellectual atmosphere in the senior public service. The touchstone for every idea is and has to be, "will it work?" Moreover, this test of practicality is applied more rigorously in Ottawa than elsewhere because political as well as economic considerations have to be given due weight.

In one sense, of course, public servants do not concern themselves with "politics". That is, they do not concern themselves with party politics. All my senior public servant colleagues were selected on the basis of their qualifications and most of them had come up through the ranks. There were virtually no what-might-be-called political appointments. Indeed, with one or two exceptions, I hadn't the slightest idea of my colleagues' political persuasions, or if they had any. Clifford Clark, himself, had been appointed by Bennett and became one of the most trusted advisers of the Liberal regime. Graham Towers, too, was appointed Governor of the Bank of Canada by Bennett and was re-appointed by King and St. Laurent.

In another sense, however, the senior advisers to the Ministers must be interested in "politics". If they are to be any good at all, they should give advice to their Ministers on all the implications of proposals under consideration, including political implications. The Ministers themselves, of course, are the final authorities on political acceptability. They make the decisions and take the consequences, good or bad.

Although the permanent senior public servant has no political axe to grind, it is his duty to support his Minister by giving him the best advice of which he is capable and by ensuring that the decisions ultimately reached are put into proper effect. To put it more shortly, the good public servant tries to keep his Minister out of trouble. This is not only the tradition of Canadian public service, but it rests upon the very practical consideration that the Department cannot be divorced from the Minister. If the Minister is successful, the Departmental officials bask in the reflected glory. If the Minister blunders, the Department has often the unenviable job of helping to straighten out the mess. If the public servant does his job properly and the Minister knows how to use him, a close relationship of mutual respect, even friendship, is bound to arise between them, which has nothing to do with party politics. It may even happen that the best "political" advice a Minister receives, in the sense of adding to his public reputation, comes from his non-political advisers.

I have often thought that this is really one of the most effective arguments for the merit system in public service appointments. The Minister who appoints political supporters to jobs at the top level in his Department is cutting himself off from good advice. The political appointee, being dependent upon the Minister for his job, is likely to tell the Minister what he thinks the Minister would like to hear, not what he should hear. A civil servant, appointed on merit and having security of tenure, gives disinterested advice, without fear or favour. The Minister does not have to accept that advice but at least he knows it has no ulterior motive, which cannot be said of much of the advice freely available to those in positions of authority.

I overheard a conversation one day between a Minister of the Crown and one of his constituency friends. This friend was asking the Minister how he ran his Department. "I suppose", he said, "you call in your Deputy Minister, tell him what you want done, and he goes and does it." The Minister, who was an honest man, replied: "No, that is not at all how it happens. I call in the Deputy Minister, tell him what the problem is and he brings forward a number of possible solutions. Then I make the decision and he carries it out." That Minister was not only honest; he knew how to use his advisers to best advantage. He left himself free for the major political tasks of decision making, leadership in Parliament and getting re-elected.

Civil servants do not make policy, all rumours to the contrary notwithstanding; that is the prerogative of the elected representatives of the people. But in this day and age, civil servants do have a profound influence upon the making of policy. In the first place, someone must assemble the relevant facts and analyze their significance. The Ministers simply do not have time to do so regardless of how many hours they work. Nor can Ministers depend entirely upon non-governmental advisers for the facts and their analysis, however useful this kind of contribution may be from time to time. When decisions are to be made, the Ministers have to be sure that the facts are really facts and the analysis unbiased.

This function of fact gathering and analysis is an important facet of the policy-making functions of the public service. But it is by no means the whole story. Senior public servants are and should be the source of ideas. Their job is to present to Ministers well considered plans of action, not only in response to requests for advice, but even before Ministers have even thought that anything needed to be done.

This should be obvious but I don't think it is. The typical senior civil servant seems to be thought of as a quite intelligent but passive agent of government, waiting to be set in motion by his Minister and producing in time a memorandum of well-balanced pros and cons. There are occasions, of course, when the senior adviser has to perform exactly that function. But when I think back over my experience, I remember more occasions when civil servants by fruitful initiatives led the Government to adopt lines of policy which would never have occurred to them otherwise.

Perhaps you have heard the story about Winston Churchill's first Ministerial appointment. Someone is said to have overheard a conversation between Mr. Churchill, as he then was, and his permanent secretary – corresponding to our Deputy Minister – who had been Head of the Department for some years. Mr. Churchill is speaking: "I know, Sir Edward, that you are the Permanent Secretary, and I am only the Minister, but at least I think that you should give some consideration to my views."

This is probably an apocryphal story and could never happen in Canada. It most certainly does not represent the attitude of the present permanent heads of Departments in Ottawa who, from my observation, behaved in a most exemplary manner when the change of Government occurred in 1957. For the sake of good government in Canada, however, there should be a better appreciation of the important role of senior civil servants. We are more dependent upon them than most of us realize. Fortunately the standard at Ottawa is, on the whole, excellent, largely because of the high ideals and strong personalities of those who laid the foundations of the present structure.

It will take continuing effort to maintain that standard. The Civil Service Act [now the Public Service Employment Act] does not, by itself, assure a competent service. It is essentially a protection against politics in the civil service. Positive recruitment must be carried on and a career in the civil service must be made to appeal as an opportunity and a challenge to the best brains among our young people.

# 12 The Bureaucratic Elite and Formation of Canadian Foreign Policy*

**James Eayrs**

It is a paradox of bureaucratic history that no sooner had the principle of an official, permanent and neutral public service been firmly established in the constitutions of Western democracies than the line between political and administrative activity began to be so smudged and blurred that today it is doubtful whether a frontier exists, let alone whether the boundary may be precisely delimited. No sophisticated student of politics is any longer shocked by this, nor does he hanker for a golden age of administration from which patronage and politics have been forever banished. The day of "the administrative eunuch with neither policies nor politics"[1] is over, if it had ever dawned; the administration of things, in splendid defiance of the Marxian prediction, has come to mean the government of men. The civil servant, more especially the senior civil servant, has been drawn ever more intimately to the centre of the political process. The range and complexity of technologies modern governments must master, the wants of citizens grown accustomed to their welfare state, the trend toward mobilized if not garri-

---

* James Eayrs, *The Art of the Possible* (Toronto, University of Toronto Press, 1961), pp. 32-38 (reprinted by permission of author and publisher). On pages 38 to 69 of his book, Professor Eayrs examines in greater detail the functions and influence of senior public servants in the Department of External Affairs.
[1] J. E. Hodgetts, "The Civil Service and Policy Formation," *Canadian Journal of Economics and Political Science*, Vol. 23, No. 4 (November, 1957), p. 471.

soned communities in an era that is neither war nor peace, all have increased his influence upon affairs.

In Canada, the senior civil servant's involvement in the policy process has been as close and continuous as anywhere in the world. The longevity of governments has brought him into prolonged and often familiar contact with political superiors. The state's uninhibited participation in taming and harnessing the resources of the more forbidding half of the continent has placed a premium upon his managerial talents. The still more specialized problems of defence in the missile age have cast doubt upon the validity of the classical formula "layman on top, expert on tap" to the extent that the political layman is concerned about national, as distinct from his own, survival. Such are the circumstances offering the senior Canadian administrator a position of power and influence greater, perhaps, than that of his counterpart in other democratic bureaucracies. Students of the political process in Canada are all agreed upon his importance, if they are just beginning to penetrate the mysteries of decision-making in which he is so crucially involved.

It might be thought, as a result of the waning influence of the career diplomatist, that the senior Canadian administrator exerts his authority only on questions of internal policy. This would be a major misinterpretation of his role. For at the summit of the civil service the divisions between foreign and domestic affairs all but disappear. At this exalted level the gaze of the civil servant sweeps across the whole horizon of public policy. Thus the senior members of the Department of External Affairs, with their commanding position on interdepartmental committees and their unique relationship with the Prime Minister's office, are assured of opportunity to influence decisions in areas far more extensive than a recital of their nominal responsibilities might suggest. In the same way, key members from other departments and agencies of government bring their experience to bear upon problems of external policy which in a more rigid division of labour would be the sole prerogative of foreign offices. The mutuality of these intrusions helps to allay the resentment they might otherwise arouse.

The group whose members stray so frequently into each other's jurisdictions is not and could not be a large one. Its numbers have varied over the years: perhaps a dozen or so in 1945, perhaps triple that by 1961. It is a group without fixed composition, just as it is a group without defined duties. Within it are usually to be found the deputy ministers and on occasion the associate and assistant deputy ministers of certain important departments – External Affairs, Finance, National Defence, Trade and Commerce, Transport – together with the senior officials of the Bank of Canada, the secretary of the Cabinet, perhaps the principal private secretary of the Prime Minister. Its members have been described as an "under Cabinet."[2] It is an apt term, for this is the group to which responsible ministers of the Crown turn, individually and collectively, for continuous advice and guidance on matters of high policy. It thus comprises a kind of civil service ministry, and to its members might well be applied Sir James Stephen's description of higher public servants in England a century ago, "statesmen in disguise."

Below the "under Cabinet" may be found a larger group of officials, usually of the rank of assistant deputy minister or head of a major branch or division, likewise engaged in general administration and properly described as members of the senior civil service. The number of such officials has greatly increased over the years – indeed the whole group is largely a product of the period since the end of the Second World War – but it is still a small and select sector of the public service as a whole. Its present membership has been estimated variously as between 150 and 250.[3] It may be best described as "the bureaucratic élite." To identify its members with the "under Cabinet" would be to exaggerate their responsibilities, but it is from the bureaucratic élite that "under Cabinets" of the future are recruited.

Where departmental divisions are barriers rather than aids to action, the "under Cabinet" and the bureaucratic élite usefully dissolve them. This may be done by the interdepartmental committee, meeting at the level of deputy ministers or heads of division, habitual resort to which is so distinctive a feature of public administration in Canada. But the interdepartmental committee as such cannot be expected to secure that broad comprehension of national interest which is its ostensible purpose and which it may achieve at its best. At its worst, however, it is a forum for departmental lobbying, for postponement and procrastination, for pitching discussion and decision at the lowest common denominator of understanding and agreement.

A valuable aid to interdepartmental liaison of a more helpful kind is

---

[2] R. Barry Farrel, "The Planning and Conduct of Foreign Policy in Canada," an unpublished Ph.D. thesis, Harvard University, 1952, p. 68.

[3] Keith B. Callard, *Advanced Administrative Training in the Public Service* (Toronto, University of Toronto Press, 1958), p. 22, cites a figure of "possibly . . . 150". John Porter, "Higher Public Servants and the Bureaucratic Elite in Canada", *Canadian Journal of Economics and Political Science*, Vol. 24, No. 4 (November, 1958), p. 499, offers a larger estimate more carefully computed. Taking as his bureaucratic universe "twenty-one deputy ministers, and twenty others at the deputy minister level; twenty-nine associate and assistant deputies, and sixty others at that level; seventy-seven below these ranks . . . at the director level . . .; and senior executives of Crown Corporations," Professor Porter arrives at a figure of 243. Of these 202 offered fairly uniform biographical data, and these officials form his "bureaucratic élite".

the practice of posting key officials to other departments and receiving in return key officials from them. "We feel that in many cases these officials are interchangeable," Mr. L. S. St. Laurent remarked soon after becoming Prime Minister, "and can be moved to new posts either in other departments or with special government agencies."[4] The practice seems to have been inaugurated during the Second World War among actual or prospective members of the "under Cabinet," and since then two or three very senior civil servants indeed have rotated every three or four years among the most important administrative posts – the under secretaryship of state for External Affairs, clerkship of the Privy Council, chairmanship of the Civil Service Commission. It has also been encouraged within the ranks of the less senior bureaucratic élite, particularly among the Departments of External Affairs, Trade and Commerce, and Finance. But civil servants who find useful experience in departments other than their own are still the exception, and the characteristic complaint continues to be the classical complaint that the public service offers rather less than private enterprise the opportunity to make the most of one's talents in whatever branch they are most urgently needed or best rewarded. Canada has developed more hesitantly than United States business the interchangeable executive along with the interchangeable part, moving imperturbably and effectively from one enterprise to the next, the interchangeable civil servant is as yet an ideal and in some quarters he is not yet that. "It seems to me that the Canadian service is much too highly fragmented," a former member of the "under Cabinet" commented in 1957. "There are far too many pigeon holes and blind alleys. . . . Too much talent gets lost and frustrated within these narrow confines. . . . I expect someone will say, 'Look at yourself. You seem to have got around.' That is true, but I have resigned three times."[5]

Perhaps the chief catalyst of co-ordination at the higher levels of the civil service is the way its members spend time together outside their offices, "having lunch at the Chateau, or on a Saturday at Madame Burger's."[6] A former member of the "under Cabinet" has stressed the importance of this extra-bureaucratic environment:

In informal gatherings at lunch, at dinner, at receptions, at evening

---

[4] *Ottawa Journal* (July 21, 1949).

[5] J. J. Deutsch, "Some Thoughts on the Public Service," *Canadian Journal of Economics and Political Science,* Vol. 23, No. 1 (February, 1957), pp. 85-86.

[6] Callard, *op. cit.,* p. 1. "The Chateau" is the Chateau Laurier Hotel, "Madame Burger's" a restaurant in Hull, Quebec, a few minutes' drive across the Ottawa River. A typical meeting of this kind was described in 1942 by the American Minister in Ottawa who having attempted without success to track down some members of the "bureaucratic élite" at the Rideau Club on the previous day, "tried my luck at the [Chateau Laurier] cafeteria today and lunched with Jack Pickersgill

parties and at the fishing club, the leading advisers of the Government . . . make a practice of consultation. . . . It is taken for granted at most Ottawa social gatherings that the wives gravitate to one end of the room while their husbands collect at the other for that infinitely fascinating occupation of "talking shop". From observation and from conversation with civil servants in other countries, I have come to the conclusion that this close contact and constant exchange of views among leading civil servants in Ottawa is in many respects unique. In Washington interdepartmental consultation hardly exists except in formally constituted committees. In London there is greater informality during working hours than in Washington, but after hours civil servants depart for their homes in widely separated suburbs of the city and have relatively few social contacts.[7]

The system works effectively enough to cure the usual bureaucratic malaise of dissipating rivalry and competition, but in doing so it may produce undesirable side-effects. The senior civil servant may view such a vast panorama of government business that he becomes incapable of that close scrutiny of detail or that specialized knowledge without which no enterprise, public or private, can fully succeed. A member of Parliament has described senior public servants in Canada as "a bunch of mandarins who, by being all-around gentlemen, sort of crossword puzzle experts, have never got around to having enough expert knowledge in any one sector to develop or elaborate policy."[8] The description is doubtless overdrawn, but it suggests a tendency of which the "mandarins" themselves are not unaware. Another hazard is that debate between spokesmen of different departments may be sapped by familiarity or inhibition. Professor Wheare has written convincingly of the need in effective committee work for the talents "of being unable to see the sense in what is being done, of questioning the whole basis of organization, of brushing difficulties aside, of ignoring logical argument, and of pressing a point beyond what most men consider a reasonable limit."[9] These are not the ordinary bureaucratic virtues, and they are likely to be in acutely short supply in a bureaucracy whose members (to adapt the famous phrase of Jinnah) occasionally intermarry and habitually interdine. The extent to which close personal association

---

(Private Secretary to the Prime Minister), Jim Coyne (Assistant to Donald Gordon in Price Control), Saul Rae and Escott Reid of the Department of External Affairs". Nancy Harvison Hooker, ed., *The Moffat Papers* (Cambridge, Mass., Harvard University Press, 1956), p. 382. The luncheon yielded more political information for the Minister than half-a-dozen formal interviews.

[7] Mitchell Sharp, "Reflections of a Former Civil Servant," reproduced above as "The Bureaucratic Elite and Policy Formation," pp. 82-87.

[8] Douglas Fisher, *Debates* (Commons) (May 24, 1960), p. 4, 184.

[9] K. C. Wheare, *Government by Committee* (Oxford, Clarendon Press, 1955), pp. 23-24.

of the members of the senior civil service makes for a dangerously monolithic approach to public policy is hard to determine. One of the members of the group has recalled after leaving it that "on many matters it was considered undesirable to try to reach common views for presentation to the Minister. . . . To have attempted to do so might have given a quite unjustified authority to the resulting piece of paper or have glossed over differences of interpretation that Ministers . . . should be aware of."[10] Against this encouraging testimony may be set the disturbing evidence of the former chairman of the Chiefs of Staff Committee that the Committee had been " 'packed' to protect the government against the receipt of unpalatable advice, rather than present the military case objectively and fearlessly on its merits."[11]

Related to this danger is another which might be called, however inelegantly, the "politicization" of the senior civil servant. It is of course a commonplace that the senior civil servant can no more avoid politics that he can avoid policy; nor is it desirable that he should. "In the formulation of policy," writes Professor Wheare, "a Higher Civil Servant is advising and assisting a Minister not only to carry through a policy which is the policy of a majority party in the House of Commons, but also to defend that policy against the criticisms and attacks of the party or parties in opposition. He works in the midst of party politics. He must be aware of party politics; indeed he ignores it at his peril. A first requirement of a Higher Civil Servant is a political sense."[12] Yet no aspect of his work requires more discretion or carries greater risk. An obsessive concern with party politics displayed under a single government over a long period of time may tempt him to place the party before the public interest; or if he is not so tempted a new set of political masters may regard him notwithstanding as too closely associated with the old to be of much use to them. "The one thing that I don't like," Mackenzie King wrote in his diary on the occasion of appointing General A. G. L. McNaughton as commander of the Canadian Army in 1939, "is the school from which he comes, which was the school of MacBrien, of Bennett, and Herridge. . . . No better evidence could be given of our disinterested action than in giving this command to one who comes . . . from that particular group."[13]

---

10 Mitchell Sharp, "Reflections of a Former Civil Servant," reproduced above as "The Bureaucratic Elite and Policy Formation," pp. 82-87.

11 Lt.-Gen. G. G. Simonds, "Where We've Gone Wrong on Defense," *Maclean's Magazine* (June 23, 1956).

12 K. C. Wheare, *The Civil Service in the Constitution* (London, London University Press, 1954), pp. 27-28.

13 J. W. Pickersgill, *The Mackenzie King Record, I, 1939-1944* (Toronto, University of Toronto Press, 1960), p. 38.

The quasi-political nature of the services rendered by senior Canadian administrators to the politicians set in authority over them is recognized by the special manner of their appointment. Unlike other civil servants, who are appointed by the Public Service Commission, deputy ministers are called to their exalted positions by the Governor-in-Council on the advice of the Prime Minister. An incoming administration is thus not only able but to some extent expected to reappraise its predecessor's "under Cabinet" in the light of its own intended policies, and to replace any obvious misfits by officials enjoying its confidence and eager to do its bidding. It would be altogether improper to regard this procedure as a throwback to the patronage system of Laurier's day and a major exception to the principles of civil service neutrality and permanence. If it results in changes of personnel, those changes are expected to be few and obvious. But following the General Election of 1957 which returned the Conservative party to power after twenty-two years in opposition, the belief was widespread that the "under Cabinet" which had served Liberal masters for so long and so well (not least of its services being to contribute from its ranks the Secretary of State for External Affairs and the Minister of Citizenship and Immigration)[14] would prove unacceptable to the new Government. Distinguished heads, it was confidently predicted, would soon roll; indeed, in some quarters the cry was that they should be made to roll, *The Globe and Mail* of Toronto arguing after the impressive Diefenbaker victory in 1958 that the time had come for "the dismantlement of what has come to be called, in Ottawa, the 'Establishment'."[15] But while some senior officials left the public service after the new administration took over, there is no evidence that any were actually dismissed. The transition, in retrospect, took place with far less friction and recrimination than had been expected, and such desire as there may have been to replace members of the "Establishment" found an outlet in the hiring of new personnel rather than in the firing of the old.[16]

---

14 Respectively, Mr. Lester Pearson (who had been Under Secretary of State for External Affairs at the time of his entering politics), and Mr. J. W. Pickersgill (previously Clerk of the Privy Council). In 1948, in announcing Mr. Pearson's Cabinet appointment, the Prime Minister remarked that the civil service should be regarded as "the stepping stone to the Ministry," a doctrine immediately stigmatized by a leading constitutional authority as asserting "a constitutional principle as novel as it is subversive of parliamentary government" and, later, as "untrue, vicious, and unnecessary." Eugene Forsey, "Mr. King and Parliamentary Government," *Canadian Journal of Economics and Political Science,* Vol. 17, No. 4 (November, 1951), p. 454.
15 *The Globe and Mail* (April 9, 1958), "The Government and the Establishment".
16 *Financial Post* (January 9, 1960), "Naming of Deputy Minister: Tricky Political Question".

# 13 The Political Rights and Activities of Canadian Public Servants*

## W. D. Kenneth Kernaghan

Until the 1960's, the approach of the Canadian federal and provincial governments to the extension of political rights to public servants was much less progressive than that of many other industrialized, democratic states. Despite the loosening of restraints on the political activity of Canadian federal employees in recent years, the conclusion of a comparative study conducted by a United States Government commission in 1967 was that

> Canadian restrictions of the political activities of civil servants have been stricter than those found in other British Commonwealth nations of comparable development, such as Australia and New Zealand, and are presently far stricter than the regulations in Great Britain itself.[1]

Canadian literature on this important and controversial topic is virtually non-existent. This brief paper will introduce the subject through an inquiry into the theoretical debate on the granting of political rights to government personnel; a comparative analysis of the legal regulations in certain foreign states and Canadian provinces; and an examination of the evolution of political rights at the federal level of government in Canada.

---

* A. M. Willms and W. D. K. Kernaghan, *Public Administration in Canada* (Toronto, Methuen Publications, 1968), pp. 446-54 (reprinted and expanded by permission of the publisher).

[1] United States, *Report of the Commission on the Political Activity of Public Personnel*, Vol. 2 (Washington, D.C., United States Government Printing Office, 1968), p. 162.

In its application to the public service, the term *political rights* generally encompasses the rights to vote, to campaign in support of a candidate, to attend political meetings, to stand as a candidate in federal or provincial elections, to hold local office and to appeal against dismissal arising from real or alleged political activity. In addition, the citizen's crucial right to freedom of expression on political matters touches on the propriety of a public servant's action in criticizing government policy in the press or from the platform and in disclosing official information without authorization.

The dilemma posed by the question of political rights for government personnel is the need to reconcile the necessity for the political neutrality and administrative impartiality of public servants with the demand for equal rights for all citizens in a democratic state. The traditional arguments promoting the extension or limitation of the political rights of government employees are offered on behalf of the general citizenry, the political heads of executive departments, political parties and the public servants themselves.

Opponents to broadening the range of political rights assert, first of all, that overt political partisanship among government employees undermines public confidence in the impartial conduct of the nation's business. Moreover, they contend that the unabated expansion of the bureaucracy's influence in the policy-making process requires a public service free of political bias. Governments can discharge their responsibilities effectively and efficiently only if the bureaucracy is divorced from partisan affiliation since the political executive, who relies on administrative subordinates for counsel and policy implementation, must be assured of their integrity and loyalty. It may be argued further that government employees should not publicly criticize government policy, whether this criticism is based on knowledge available to the general public or on information available to public servants by virtue of their official position. Certainly, in the interests of state security, governments must impose heavy penalties on public servants who make unauthorized use of official documents. Another common argument for the restriction of political rights is that in accepting the advantages of security and generous fringe benefits accompanying government employment, public servants can realistically be expected to relinquish certain political rights enjoyed by other citizens. Finally, public servants must be protected against financial exploitation or coercion by a superior with party affiliations who can affect his subordinates' prospects for promotion.

On the other hand, advocates of the emancipation of public servants from political restraints are motivated in large part by the political sterilization of an increasing percentage of the population as the number of public servants continues to expand.[2] In a democratic society, the isolation of such a substantial proportion of the population from political activity must be offset by substantive and demonstrable benefits to the public interest. An especially powerful argument for the removal of political restrictions is that the public services contain a concentration of the best educated and best informed persons in the country. As a consequence of excessive limitations on the political rights of public personnel, the nation may be deprived not only of an articulate and knowledgeable expression of views on public issues but also of talented persons reluctant to accept employment which restricts their political activities. In addition, political parties may be obliged to exclude from active party membership and possible candidature persons whose intimate acquaintance with governmental problems is invaluable to the formulation of party policy.

The solution to this conflict between administrative nonpartisanship and the enjoyment of political rights is not a simple weighing of these opposing theoretical considerations or the application of one or the other set of arguments to particular countries. In practice, it is common for governments to evolve a position of compromise between the unworkable extremes of unrestrained political activity and absolute political sterilization. The measure of political activity accorded government employees in democratic societies may be depicted along a continuum between these two extreme poles.

On this continuum, the status of public servants in the United States approaches the extremity of complete exclusion from political activity. The *Hatch Act* of 1939 and its amendment in 1940[3] severely restrict the political activities of more than 4.5 million public servants at the federal, state and local levels of government.[4] The provisions of this federal statute apply to employees of state and local governments working on programs financed wholly or in part by federal loans or grants.

The narrow range of permissible political activities under the Act includes the right to vote; the right to express views "on all political subjects and candidates"[5]; membership in political party clubs and attendance at political rallies and conventions; voluntary contributions to

---

[2] The number of public servants at all levels of Canadian government today amounts to 17.2 per cent or about one sixth of the total labor force. See my article "An Overview of Public Administration in Canada Today", Canadian Public Administration, Vol. 11, No. 3 (Fall, 1968), pp. 292-93.
[3] 53 United States, *Statutes,* 1147 (1939) and 54 United States, *Statutes,* 767, (1940).
[4] *Report of the Commission on the Political Activity of Public Personnel, op. cit.,* Vol. 1, p. 11.
[5] The United States Civil Service Commission has explained that this right "is subject to the prohibition that employees may not take any active part in political management or in political campaigns". *Political Activity of Federal Officers and Employees,* United States Civil Service Commission (Washington, D.C., May, 1966), pamphlet 20, p. 12.

political parties and organizations; wearing political badges and display-
ing political stickers and signs on a car or at a home; participation in local
non-partisan elections; and full political activity on matters "relating to
constitutional amendments, referendums, approval of municipal ordi-
nances, and others of a similar character".

A wider range of prohibited activities includes standing as a candidate
for federal, state or local office; organizing or holding office in a political
club; serving as a speaker, delegate or alternate to a party convention;
campaigning actively for a political party or candidate through public
speeches, the distribution of literature, the circulation of nominating
petitions or participation in parades; engaging in official or partisan activity at the polls on election day or transporting voters to the polls; and
soliciting political contributions. The penalty imposed for violation of
these prohibitions is removal from office or suspension without pay for a
minimum period of 30 days.

The Commission on the Political Activity of Public Personnel, appointed jointly by the President and both Houses of Congress in 1966,
presented a three-volume report recommending the removal of many of
the existing barriers to political activity.[6] The implementation of these
recommendations would help to eliminate numerous abuses of the *Hatch
Act* which have arisen partly from uncertainty among public servants as to
the permissible and proscribed activities under the Act. One of the central
proposals of the Commission was that "the law regulating political activity
of government personnel should specify in readily understandable terms
those political activities which are prohibited, and specifically permit all
others."[7]

The British Government's attitude on the issue of political activity for
public servants brings their position closer to the pole of unrestrained
political activity. Yet this general statement must be severely qualified
since a substantial number of British civil servants are barred from all but
the most limited political activity. Following an evolution over 80 years
in the direction of extending the scope of political activity, a reconciliation
of views contained in the Masterman Committee Report[8] with the
counter-proposal of the staff side of a Whitley Council Committee led to
the adoption in 1953 of a differentiated system of political rights for civil
servants.[9]

---

6 See especially Vol. 1, *Findings and Recommendations.*
7 *Ibid.*, p. 4.
8 Great Britain, *Report of the Committee on the Political Activities of Civil Servants* (London, His Majesty's Stationery Office, 1949), Cmd. 7718 (June, 1949).
9 *The Political Activities of Civil Servants* (London, Her Majesty's Stationery
Office, 1953), Cmd. 8783 (March, 1953). See also *Establishment Circular* 26/53
(Treasury, August 14, 1953).

The entire body of British civil servants was divided into three major categories labelled *politically free, intermediate* and *politically restricted* depending on their influence on policy making and their occupational relationships with the public. The politically free category comprises all employees working in the industrial civil service and those in the non-industrial civil service falling within the manipulative grades of the post office and the minor grades of messengers and cleaners. These civil servants are free to participate fully in national and local political activities although they must submit their resignations before nomination day if they stand for election. Moreover, they may be subsequently reinstated to the civil service on the fulfilment of certain conditions. The intermediate category embraces those civil servants performing clerical and typing responsibilities. These employees may take part in all political activities except candidacy for Parliament. Their political activities are subject, however, to the granting of departmental permission "according to the degree and nature of the conduct with the public involved"[10] and to the acceptance of a code of discretion. The politically restricted category includes all other civil servants, that is, those falling within the executive, the professional, the scientific and technical, and the administrative grades. Members of this restricted category will normally be permitted to take part in local political activities which are not associated with national political organizations. The political activities of this group are subject both to the acceptance of a code of discretion and the obligation to inform the department of election to a local government office.

The location of Canada's federal public servants on the continuum of political activity lies between the positions of the United States and Great Britain. Only during the decade of the 1960's did Canada take the progressive measures necessary to achieve this status.

For 40 years following Confederation, the Canadian federal government was plagued by a heritage of patronage from the pre-Confederation era of colonial rule. The practices of appointment for party service, the use of government employees to promote partisan objectives, the holding of office at pleasure and rotation in office brought the government to the verge of the United States *spoils system*. Little advance toward the elimination of the evils of patronage was made before the *Civil Service Amendment Act* of 1908[11] which applied the merit principle to the inside service (civil servants in Ottawa) and imposed the penalty of dismissal for political activity. Patronage in the outside service continued apace, however, and the device of making temporary appointments on political grounds

---

10 *Ibid.,* sec. 37(b).
11 *Statutes,* 7-8 Edw. VII, c. 15.

to the inside service almost destroyed the merit system during the following decade.

Then, in 1918, a new *Civil Service Act*[12] extended the merit system. Provision was made for admission by competitive examination to both the inside and outside services. The prohibition against political activity was reinforced by vesting exclusive power of appointment and promotion in the Civil Service Commission rather than in the politicians. Section 55 of the Act, which stood unaltered for 43 years, stated that

1. No deputy head, officer, clerk or employee in the Civil Service shall be debarred from voting at any Dominion or provincial election if, under the laws governing the said election, he has the right to vote; but no such deputy head, officer, clerk or employee shall engage in partisan work in connection with any such election, or contribute, receive or in any way deal with any money for any party funds.

2. Any person violating any of the provisions of this section shall be dismissed from the Civil Service.

Although the enforcement of the Act diminished substantially the magnitude of partisan political activity among government employees, Dawson wrote as late as 1936 that "political patronage is still the great enemy of civil service efficiency in Canada".[13]

Nevertheless, the effect of patronage on appointments to positions falling under the authority of the Civil Service Commission gradually dwindled to the point where by 1960, Hughes, then chairman of the Commission, could write that

... no one will seriously contend that the influence of political patronage in the recruitment and selection of public employees is not on the decline. Even in those jurisdictions where there are no statutory safeguards against its operation, there is a general inclination to avoid it and at the very least to pay lip-service to the principle of appointment and promotion by merit.[14]

In making reference to "those jurisdictions where there are no statutory safeguards," Hughes was alluding to the large numbers of public servants working in government positions and agencies which had over the years been exempted from the application of the inflexible and overcentralized controls of the *Civil Service Act*. Indeed, in 1960, only 131,953 persons out of a total civilian public service of 344,362 (less than 40 per cent)

---

[12] *Ibid.*, 8-9 Geo. V, c. 12.

[13] R. M. Dawson, "The Canadian Civil Service," *Canadian Journal of Economics and Political Science,* Vol. 2 (August, 1936), p. 291.

[14] S. H. S. Hughes, "The Public Officials—Parliament, the Public and the Press," *Canadian Public Administration,* Vol. 3, No. 4 (December, 1960), p. 295.

were subject to the provisions of the Act, including the restrictions on political activity.[15] Although the acceptance of the merit principle by exempt groups varies from agency to agency, political appointments and activities have been more common outside the confines of the *Civil Service Act*.

Also in 1960, the federal government, by Order-in-Council, conceded a public servant the legal right to participate in political movements and elections at the local level of government "if he has been granted leave without pay to do so or if his Deputy Minister finds that holding such office will not prevent the civil servant from properly discharging his duties. . . ."[16] A federal public servant may in addition receive leave without pay if he wins election to a full-time municipal office.[17]

The Province of Saskatchewan long preceded the federal government in removing certain deterrents to the political activity of public employees. As early as 1947, the Saskatchewan government bestowed on its employees generous political privileges. *The Public Service Act*[18] provides that no public servant may engage in political activity during working hours; use his authority to coerce any other employee into political participation or to make financial contributions to any political party; or indulge in political activities which might "impair his usefulness in the position in which he is employed". Aside from these minor restraints, the province's public servants are free to take part in political activity outside their regular working hours. Furthermore, a government employee who wishes to stand for public office may have 30 days leave of absence without pay before election day.

The 1958 *Report of the Civil Service Commission on Personnel Administration in the Public Service*[19] (the Heeney *Report*) proposed few modifications in federal legislation affecting political activity. The *Report* included proposals that public servants be permitted to act as poll officials under specified conditions and that a commission of inquiry be established to consider alleged instances of political partisanship. The revision of the *Civil Service Act*[20] in 1961 retained the longstanding prohibition against partisan work but incorporated the recommendation of the Heeney *Report* that an alleged violation of political activity be the subject of an

---

15 Civil Service Commission, *Annual Report*, 1960 (Ottawa, Queen's Printer, 1961), Appendix B, *Composition of the Public Service as of September 30, 1960*, p. 34.

16 *Public Office—Municipal or Civic*, P.C. 1960—1121, August 12, 1960 (Ottawa, Queen's Printer).

17 *Civil Service Regulations*, c. 71. *Canada Gazette*, Vol. 96, No. 7 (Ottawa, April 11, 1962), p. 396.

18 Saskatchewan, *Revised Statutes*, 1965, c. 9, sec. 52.

19 (Ottawa, Queen's Printer, December, 1958), pp. 93-94.

20 Canada, *Statutes*, c. 57.

inquiry. In all provinces except Saskatchewan, Ontario and Quebec, legal regulations or established practices affecting political activity are today identical or very similar to the federal procedure as is existed under this 1961 Act. The federal government was upstaged by the 1963 amendments to Ontario's *Public Service Act*[21] which liberalized previous regulations in the realm of political activity for a large proportion of the province's employees. Any public servant, other than deputy ministers and certain designated senior officials, may be a candidate or actively support another candidate for election to municipal office providing that such activity does not adversely affect the employee's performance on the job; does not harm the interests of the Crown; and is not affiliated with a provincial or federal political party. The employee shall, however, be granted a leave of absence without pay to stand for provincial or federal election or to campaign openly and to solicit funds in support of a provincial or federal party. An Ontario public servant who resigns on winning election may be reinstated if he ceases to be a political representative within five years and applies for reappointment within the subsequent three months.

During the period between these amendments to the Act and October 29, 1968, six Ontario public servants (3 Conservatives, 2 Liberals and 1 New Democrat) sought election to *federal* office and all were defeated. Of three officials (2 Conservatives, and 1 New Democrat) standing for *provincial* office, two (both Conservatives) were elected.[22]

According to the terms of the Quebec *Civil Service Act*,[23] a provincial civil servant may participate in federal or provincial political activities only on resignation from the civil service. If defeated in an electoral contest, the civil servant is entitled to reappointment to the service.

On the basis of the recommendations of a joint committee of the House of Commons and the Senate on employer-employee relations in the federal public service,[24] significant alterations in federal legislation regulating political activities were incorporated in the *Public Service Employment Act*.[25] Public servants are now permitted to attend political meetings and to contribute money to a candidate's campaign or to party coffers. The Public Service Commission has authority to approve requests for leave of absence without pay to enable any employee to seek nomination and election to federal, provincial or municipal office. These requests may be denied if the employee's usefulness would be impaired by such activity.

---

[21] Ontario, *Statutes*, 1961-1962, c. 121 as amended by *Statutes*, 1962-1963, c. 118.
[22] The author extends appreciation to officials of the Ontario Civil Service Commission for making these statistics available.
[23] Quebec, *Statutes*, 1965, c. 14.
[24] Ottawa, Queen's Printer, 1966-1967.
[25] Canada, *Statutes*, 1966-1967, c. 71.

Furthermore, in the event of election to office, the employee automatically vacates his position.

The first test of the new regulations came during the federal election of June 25, 1967. [26] The Public Service Commission approved sixteen of seventeen requests for permission to seek nomination as a candidate. Permission was denied a personnel administrator engaged in recruitment and selection for his Department on the grounds that his candidacy would impair his usefulness to the Public Service. Eight of the sixteen candidates were nominated (5 Liberals, 2 New Democrats and 1 Conservative) and three candidates (all Liberals) were elected.

Under section 32(6) of the Act, the Commission may conduct an inquiry into alleged contraventions of the regulations and recommend dismissal of an offending employee only if an "allegation is made to the Commission by a person who is or has been a candidate for election". Following the election, a few departments sought the Commission's counsel as to what measures could be taken against an employee who had worked for a candidate. The Commission advised these departments to recommend to the Treasury Board a penalty for misconduct or breach of discipline. Up to July 29, 1968, the Treasury Board had received no requests for disciplinary action.

The very general language of the statute and the inadequacy of its coverage provides little specific direction to federal employees and leaves much discretion as to acceptable and forbidden political activities to the Public Service Commission. For example, the Act makes no reference to membership in political parties. In practice, however, federal employees may hold "inactive membership" in a political party, that is, they may be seen at party gatherings and rallies but may not be heard.

None of the Canadian legislation on political activity discussed to this point has treated the critical and delicate issue of the right of public servants to freedom of expression on political matters. The traditional, but informal, practice has been that government employees should maintain "a certain reserve" in their discussion of public questions. In 1965, a federal government actuary was dismissed for his public denunciations of the *Canada Pension Plan* which at the time was being debated in the House of Commons. The Appeal Board upheld the dismissal primarily on the grounds that the employee had special responsibilities "as a member of the civil service to uphold the constitutional laws and traditions and as an employee to refrain from conducting himself in a manner that would destroy his harmonious relationship with his employer". In addition,

---

[26] The author is indebted to officials of the Public Service Commission for information related to the June 25 election.

the Board noted that the employee's conduct in making "the representatives of the press and the public . . . witnesses to the unedifying spectacle of a senior civil servant attacking government policy . . . tended to make the discharge of the government's functions more difficult".[27]

The unauthorized disclosure of information by public servants is ordinarily regulated by the initial oath or affirmation of office and secrecy.[28] Severe penalties may be imposed under the *Official Secrets Act*[29] on government employees who make unauthorized use of official information, particularly the communication of a "code word, pass word, sketch, plan, model, article, note, document or information" to agents of a foreign power.

Comparative analysis indicates that the gradual extension of political rights to certain groups of government employees is not likely to injure the public interest through the reintroduction of appointment and promotion on partisan grounds. Canadian federal and provincial governments may benefit not only from granting a broader range of political rights but from a more explicit legislative statement of permissible and prohibited political activities. Canadian governments may also evaluate the procedure of differentiating among public servants for purposes of political activity based on the British or the Ontario model.

The federal government and certain provincial governments have moved a long way in the direction of an appropriate balance between the political neutrality and the individual rights of government employees. Yet, in a comparative context, not only with Great Britain but with several developed countries in Western Europe and Asia, Canadian laws and practices appear unduly restrictive. The accumulation of much more empirical data on the extent of political activity at all levels of Canadian government is essential, however, before further legislative modifications are made.

---

[27] "Appeal of Mr. John W. Kroeker, Actuary 6 (Senior Actuary) against decision of Superintendent of Insurance to recommend dismissal under Section 60 of the Civil Service Act", INS-A-20, April 9, 1965, pp. 22-23.

[28] The federal wording is as follows: "I, (A.B.) solemnly and sincerely swear (or affirm) that I will faithfully and honestly fulfil the duties that devolve upon me by reason of my employment in the Public Service and that I will not, without due authority in that behalf, disclose or make known any matter that comes to my knowledge by reason of such employment. (In the case where an oath is taken add, 'So help me God'.)" Schedule C of the *Public Service Employment Act*.

[29] Canada, *Revised Statutes*, 1952, c. 198.

# 14 Pressure Groups and the Canadian Bureaucracy: Farm Organizations in Canada*

## Helen Jones Dawson

The major national farm organizations in Canada are the Canadian Federation of Agriculture and the National Farmers' Union. The Canadian Federation of Agriculture is the largest and most generally representative of the farm organizations. It was organized in 1935 but did not achieve any degree of influence in government circles until 1941. The national Federation, which does not have direct membership, is composed of Provincial Branches and three national commodity group affiliates. These in turn may have direct farmer members; they may be composed of various commodity groups (with or without direct farmer members); they may also include agricultural cooperatives.[1] The national body is financed by voluntary assessment of its affiliates, and lack of money has been one of its recurring problems. One of the basic weaknesses of the Federation is that its ability to represent farmers before government depends to a very large degree upon the efficiency and local prestige of the provincial branches and the performance is by no means equal. At the very best it is fair to say that the Federation, with no direct membership,

* Helen Jones Dawson, "Relations Between Farm Organizations and the Civil Service in Canada and Great Britain," *Canadian Public Administration*, Vol. 10, No. 4 (December, 1967), pp. 450-70 (reprinted and abridged by permission of author and publisher).
1 For further details, see my article "Interest Group: The Canadian Federation of Agriculture," *Canadian Public Administration*, Vol. 3, No. 2 (June, 1960), pp. 134-49.

lacks contact with the farmers; at the worst, it is possible that many farmers do not even know that it exists. This remoteness encouraged the growth of a rival farm organization, now called the National Farmers' Union. The Union started on the prairies in the 1930s, but did not present its first formal brief to the federal government until 1948. It now has branches in the three prairie provinces, British Columbia, and Ontario. It started out originally as an organization mainly interested in the welfare of cereal farmers but has now broadened its interests in accordance with its geographical expansion. It still retains its original hostility to farm cooperatives, which is one of its major points of difference with the Federation. It has direct farmer membership and offers members special insurance rates and some legal advice. Its main power lies in the provincial sphere, and the lack of a national office in Ottawa, the rather loose coordination exercised by the national organization over its provincial components, and its ideas of direct action (by which it means strikes, boycotts and marches) have severely restricted its influence in Ottawa. The two Canadian organizations have traditionally been based on regional and commodity interests. Moreover, because of the strong regional differences extant in both the Canadian organizations, they base their presentations to government upon the resolutions passed at annual meetings.

These Canadian organizations are bedevilled by both regionalism and distances, which have serious financial and administrative results. This has consequences both on the amount of pressure that can be brought to bear on politicians and civil servants and on the amount of expertise which can be applied to any given topic. The organizations do have a high degree of stability in the personnel of their governing bodies. One important consequence of this is that executive officers develop long-term relationships with civil servants. The two national organizations are competitive, however, and the smaller of the two is by no means content to be regarded as a junior partner. It takes no great imagination to realize the consequences of this for the effectiveness of the organizations in their relations with government.

The Canadian organizations have a difficult problem to overcome which stems not only from the federal nature of the country, but, even more important, from the fact that agriculture is a concurrent power of both the federal and provincial governments. This means that the Canadian organizations must maintain strong provincial organizations in order to exert pressure on provincial governments and also to a certain degree upon federal civil servants posted in the field. The problem of financing and staffing these provincial organizations is one that neither Canadian organization has yet overcome. There is also the additional and very difficult business of trying to formulate any kind of a national policy out of the disparate, and sometimes contradictory, views of their affiliates. The rapidly developing concept of cooperative federalism has increased all of these difficulties. Perhaps the ARDA program may be taken as an example. Not only must the organizations persuade the federal government that certain programs should be undertaken, but it must also persuade the provincial governments. Since the federal government signs separate agreements with each of the provinces it will be obvious that even the Federation, with four full-time officials in Ottawa, leaving aside the Farm Union with no permanent staff in Ottawa, would be hard put to keep an eye on everything. There is, however, one advantage which the Canadian organizations can gain from this diffusion of responsibility: the possibility of having the provincial organizations bring pressure to bear both upon provincial representatives in the federal cabinet and on federal civil servants in the field.

Working in a parliamentary system it is inevitable that Canadian organizations find it essential to influence policy and legislation before the parliamentary stage is reached. The achievement of minor amendments to agricultural legislation at the committee stage in Parliament has not been a productive endeavour in Canada. The Federation at least appears to have a very clear appreciation of this fact. In the mid-fifties, when finances allowed the appointment of another full-time staff member in Ottawa, his main function was to maintain contact with permanent officials in the government. The Canadian Farmers' Union still relies on periodic delegations to make its views known; it also has sponsored "Marches on Ottawa" as a form of political pressure. It would be difficult to judge whether these have more seriously annoyed the politicians or the civil servants. In any case, the Federation realizes that the most effective means of influencing policy and legislation is through constant contact and friendly relations with civil servants.

This policy, which the Federation describes as consultation and cooperation, is carried on so quietly and on such an informal basis that it is hard for an organization to claim credit for important successes. It is basically unexciting and can lead to allegations from the rank and file that the organization is not taking a sufficiently aggressive stand in pressing its claims on government. This is most clearly apparent in the case of the Federation and undoubtedly was one of the factors which gave rise to the growth of the Canadian Farmers' Union.

In examining the relationship between the agricultural interest groups and senior civil servants, it is important to remember that mutual respect and trust is the single most important factor, for without it there is no real relationship. Here as in many other aspects of political behaviour the informal relationships are often more important than the formal ones. In Canada, the formal relationships are limited in number, and this puts increased emphasis on the informal ones. The rapid development of cooperative federalism in which so many important projects are jointly administered by the federal and provincial governments also puts a premium on informal methods. In addition, the dispersal of the centre of responsibility makes it very difficult to evaluate the exact nature of the relations between the farm organizations and senior civil servants from one end of the country to the other, since a great deal of the day-to-day work is carried out by its provincial branches with both federal officials in the field and provincial civil servants.

The basis of informal consultation lies in the two-way flow of information and the exchange of ideas. The Canadian Federation of Agriculture has always worked more closely with civil servants than with politicians. The Federation has had and used many opportunities to strengthen its personal relationship with senior administrators in the federal service and particularly in the Department of Agriculture and the various boards and agencies associated with it. The necessities of wartime resulted in a rapid development of close consultation and cooperation. The Federation has continued this policy to the discontent of the more militant members in the farm community.[2] The very informality of the relationship[3] between the Federation and civil servants means that it is difficult to describe in any great detail.

The pattern of close consultation was largely established under the necessity of wartime conditions. The Federation realized that although cabinet ministers make policies, the administrators both influence the shape of the policies and execute them. The Federation tries to ensure that these officials are kept aware of the effect on farmers of the increasing number and complexity of government regulations. To this end it has worked closely with the senior administrators of several departments, notably Agriculture, Trade and Commerce, Finance, Citizenship and Immigration, Forestry and Rural Development, and Labour. In addition the Federation has developed close relationships with Crown corporations,

---

[2] In 1967, two of the Federation's most important provincial affiliates, the Ontario Federation of Agriculture and the Union Catholique des Cultivateurs, departed from long-standing Federation policy to join the Farmers' Union in a march on Ottawa.

[3] No mention has been made here of the Canadian Farmers' Union. Lacking an office in Ottawa to maintain constant contact with government officials the Union has had to rely on periodic delegations and occasional discussions when Union officials attend meetings of government advisory committees in Ottawa. Although it would hardly be accurate to say that any kind of a relationship has been built up, it is possible to detect hostility toward the Union among some officials.

especially with the broadcasting corporations. The Federation in its public statements is careful not to criticize civil servants; in fact, it is more common to find praise of departmental cooperation. Although the Federation is capable of going to the minister when it meets what it considers to be unwarranted obstacles at the administrative level, it does not make public announcements about these appeals. Thus, although the officials may not be pleased, they are not publicly exposed. The Canadian Farmers' Union has on occasion told at least its own members when concessions were granted as a result of appealing to ministers over the heads of civil servants. This inevitably causes some strain in the fabric of close consultation if the civil servants are fearful of being thus exposed to public criticism. The other point is that although the Federation has close contacts with the civil service, it does not normally work on individual complaints or cases of hardship. The Canadian Farmers' Union, lacking an office in Ottawa, does a limited amount of this type of work at the national level, but it is quite capable of requesting changes in regulations to take into account individual cases.

The farm organizations keep in close contact with the civil service in the area of amendment of existing legislation and the introduction of new legislation. There is considerable consultation while bills are still in the draft stage. The Canadian Federation does not often present draft legislation for consideration; however, some of the provincial Federations in Canada have had considerable success in this endeavour.[4] The national Federation for its part concentrates its efforts on trying to ensure that government legislation takes its views into account. Both ministers and civil servants consult the officials of the Canadian farm organizations about the broad outlines of new policies before they are submitted to Parliament.[5] It is decidedly unusual for a Canadian government to permit alteration of a bill after it has been introduced in Parliament. The Canadian Federation believes there would be very little point in trying to influence members of Parliament, favourably or otherwise. The Canadian Farmers' Union, on the other hand, while it organizes marches on Ottawa for the avowed purpose of influencing members on general issues, has not yet tried this method of exerting influence in respect to specific measures before the House.

The consultative process which takes place through the medium of advisory committees is also difficult to evaluate. In Canada, the only

---

[4] In 1956 the Federation's Board of Directors adopted a Model Farm Products Marketing Act and the statute books of several provinces now bear legislation with a marked resemblance to this model.

[5] According to the Federation of Agriculture, it was asked to make suggestions on the *first* draft of the Agricultural Stabilization Bill. *President's Annual Address,* 1958, p. 8.

advisory committee in the agricultural sphere which has had any marked degree of influence or prestige was the wartime Committee on Food. Aside from that notable exception they are viewed with a jaundiced, if cautious, eye by ministers, civil servants, and the more astute officials of the farm organizations, all for different reasons.[6] There is a growing feeling, at least among officials of the Federation, that advisory committees cannot influence policy decisions because these are firm before they are even discussed with the committees. The Canadian Farmers' Union does not appear to share these reservations.[7] In Canada there is the feeling that the personnel of advisory committees may be selected more on the basis of politics than on ability to represent the industry.[8] It is only fair to add that the lack of expertise in the Canadian farm organizations seriously hampers their ability to make substantive contributions to advisory committees. Indeed the organizations do not usually attempt to brief or consult with their officials who are appointed to advisory committees.

Whatever the reasons may be, advisory committees are not much used in Canada. Aside from the half-dozen authorized by statute, the Department of Agriculture lists seventy-six "advisory" committees, but they are with very few exceptions composed entirely of civil servants; for the most part they are of a highly technical nature.[9]

For many years Canada has had one rather public form of consultation between government and organized farm groups. This is what the newspapers are pleased to call "the Farmers' Parliament." It consists of the federal and provincial ministers of agriculture, their deputy ministers, certain other federal ministers and senior administrators, representatives of all farm organizations, and of the farm and rural press. This group meets annually in Ottawa to discuss the problems and prospects of agriculture. Although it may have been an effective medium of communications for

---

6 For details about these reservations see my article "Interest Group: The Canadian Federation of Agriculture," *op. cit.,* pp. 146-47. That assessment is corroborated to a certain extent by the fact that the advisory committee to the Agricultural Stabilization Board was not convened between September, 1962 and February, 1964 despite the fact that there is statutory provision for two meetings each year.

7 Symptomatic of the different attitude toward these committees is the fact that the Union's representative on the Advisory Committee to the Stabilization Board committed, what would in Britain be considered, a breach of confidence by revealing the stands taken by various members of the Committee. *Debates* (Commons) (April 24, 1959), p. 3,209, and (May 1, 1959), p. 3,241.

8 It is at least interesting that a member of the Advisory Committee to the Stabilization Board would need to emphasize that the personnel of the Committee had remained the same *despite* a change of government.

9 Photostatic copy of a Department of Agriculture document, n.d. This list indicates that only seven committees had personnel from outside the federal civil service and only one had representatives of farm organizations. In some cases a number of the incumbents are deceased.

the Government when the parliament was started during the early 1940's, it is doubtful if it now serves any useful purpose aside from the opportunity to develop more personal contacts in the industry. It certainly does not provide a real forum for consultation.[10]

In summary, there are two general farm organizations in Canada which do not always agree. Furthermore, neither of these have ever been able to subordinate the wishes of individual commodity groups to the need for a coherent national agricultural policy. Thus Canadian governments are frequently requested to do multitudinous, and sometimes contradictory, things for the agricultural industry. It is also quite obvious that the Canadian farm organizations suffer from immaturity. This is perhaps most obvious in the case of the Canadian Farmers' Union with its marches, tractor parades, strikes, and boycotts. It is, however, true of the Federation as well. It is, for example, unlikely that even the more sophisticated Federation could muster the finances or the expert staff necessary to face the expert civil servants of the Department of Agriculture in negotiations for an annual price review. In fact, the Federation's present relations with the civil service rests almost entirely upon an aura of trust and respect which has been built up over a number of years, not upon technical competence. Despite its immaturity in many respects the Federation has realized for many years that it can influence policy only when governments wish advice, but that it can mitigate the worst consequences of unfortunate policies by working in close conjunction with the civil service.

---

[10] The general frustration is revealed by the Farmers' Union's charge that the Conference had failed to make any concrete proposals to guide farmers in their future activities. *Debates* (Commons) (February 7, 1957), p. 1090. The Federation now intends to request the abolition of this forum.

# 15 Pressure Groups and the Canadian Bureaucracy: Scientists and Science Policy Machinery*

## G. Bruce Doern

Science has been called the operative ideology of the post-industrial state. Scientists and engineers are being recruited into all sectors of society, including the government bureaucracy, at an ever-increasing rate. Since 1945 virtually every western society has witnessed a public debate about how this latest group of experts can be fitted into the political and bureaucratic decision-making structures.[1]

Do scientists constitute a group whose potential power is qualitatively different than the other species of knowledge experts who have preceded them into government service (e.g., economists, lawyers, military experts)? Is there real substance to the C. P. Snow thesis that the humanist-political and the scientific realms constitute "two cultures" which have great difficulty communicating with one another, or that generalist politicians must avoid having scientist "overlords" as advisors?[2] The debate about the

---

* This essay is a very brief *survey* of an exceedingly complex topic. It is based on the writer's research on "Scientists and the Making of Science Policies in Canada", a Ph.D. dissertation (in progress) for the Department of Political Studies at Queen's University. Readers are referred to the above work and to other works cited below for a full account of the events and issues discussed here.
[1] For a general analysis of the problems of science and government see D. K. Price, *The Scientific Estate* (Cambridge, Mass., The Belkap Press, 1965).
[2] See C. P. Snow, *Science and Government* (Cambridge, Mass., Harvard University Press, 1961), and C. P. Snow, *The Two Cultures and a Second Look: An Expanded Version of the Two Cultures and the Scientific Revolution* (New York, Mentor Books, 1964).

power and place of science and scientists is really a part of a larger debate about the technocratic society and the capacity of generalist politicians to control and manage societies of this kind.

While the discussion has been frequently polemical and the early caricature of the "two cultures" and the "overlord" has been mellowed by the realities of the subsequent evolution of the scientist-politician relationship, the debate has always been important. It is especially topical in the contemporary Canadian context where the debate on the place of science in Canadian government and society is more lively than at any time in our history. It follows by a few years similar debates in countries like the United States, France and Britain.[3]

The Canadian debate about the scientists and the making of science policies has been generated by much the same set of forces that prevailed in other western societies. One commentator on the British debate summed up these forces very compactly:

Scientific and technological sophistication is increasingly seen as a critical factor in industrial "modernization" as well as in sheer commercial viability and national prestige. The growing recognition of the interrelatedness of science and technology with other spheres of policy, together with the spiraling costs of research equipment and the general scarcity of scientific and technical manpower, has led all countries toward broader concepts of science "planning", "programming" or "coordination".[4]

The term "science policy" has come to represent the need for scientists to be involved in two dimensions of policy – policies *for* science and science *in* policy. Policies for science include policies for the management and support of scientific manpower and resources and the allocation of research funds. Science in policy involves science as a means for solving problems in other substantive public policy areas. The two are always linked to a greater or lesser degree. This brief analysis of the role and power of Canadian scientists in both these dimensions will be made in the context of the evolution of the Canadian science policy machinery that politicians have inserted into the Canadian bureaucracy and governmental structure. The evolution of this machinery will be described *briefly* under four sections; (a) the role of the National Research Council (NRC), (b) the wartime science machinery, (c) the Glassco Commission recommendations, and (d) the role of the Science Secretariat and Science Council.

---

[3] See R. Gilpin and C. Wright, *Scientists and National Policy Making* (New York, Columbia University Press, 1964); R. Gilpin, *France in the Age of the Scientific State* (Princeton, Princeton University Press 1968); and N. J. Vig, *Science and Technology in British Politics* (Oxford, Pergamon Press, 1968).

[4] Vig, *op. cit.*, p. 2.

## (a) The Role of the National Research Council

The NRC was created by statute in 1917 as a response to the wartime need for rationalizing Canada's scientific effort.[5] It was officially an "honorary advisory council" to the Privy Council Committee on Scientific and Industrial Research (a Cabinet committee) and was charged with being a general advisor to the government concerning its science programs, especially those related to the utilization of resources (which constituted Canada's major "industrial" component).

The NRC was composed primarily of scientists and as an organization of scientists inserted into a governmental structure composed essentially of non-scientists, it spent a significant part of its early history establishing itself in the internal "political system" of the Canadian bureaucracy. Its terms of reference often brought it into jurisdictional conflict with other departments such as Agriculture, the Department of the Interior and later the Department of Mines whose basic "mission" related to the primary resource fields. For much of the 1920's and early 1930's the NRC (whose President became a full-time officer only after 1928) experienced considerable difficulty in securing its legal independence from successive Ministers of Trade and Commerce, whose perceptions of science, especially in this prolonged period of austerity and then depression, were such as to treat science in much the same way that politicians would treat any other kind of government output or expenditure.

During this period the NRC was able to exert sufficient influence to build up a program of research support for university researchers and via its network of associate committees to assist in a number of industrial research problems in the primary resources field. Its internal power over politicians or even over other scientists in the existing agencies of the federal government was, however, minimal.

## (b) The Wartime Science Machinery

From 1932 until 1939 the NRC had begun to build up its own laboratories, and, in the process, its role as advisor seemed to have been displaced by the exigencies of building its own internal organization. With the outbreak of the war the role and influence of scientists in Canada assumed an importance unequalled before (or probably since). The size

---

[5] See M. Thistle, *The Inner Ring* (Toronto, University of Toronto Press, 1965) for an account of the early role of NRC. See also *Proceedings of the Sub-Committee of the Privy Council on Scientific and Industrial Research,* NRC Office Copy, First Meeting, April 25, 1929, to Twenty-Third Meeting, August 1, 1944, inclusive.

of the scientific establishment in NRC increased from 300 in 1939 to 700 in 1945 and NRC clearly became the primary government science agency.[6]

Two aspects of the wartime experience are especially noteworthy. First, the NRC's role as science adviser became preeminent, partly because of the compulsions of war but also because of the relationship that developed between NRC's President, Dr. C. J. Mackenzie, and the Minister of Trade and Commerce, the Honorable C. D. Howe. Both were engineers and they were, in addition, close personal friends. This very personalized and compact scientist-politician relationship is one which worked exceedingly well, although it appears also to correspond to the science "overlord" about which C. P. Snow wrote so critically.[7]

The second aspect of the war experience is that the governmental science sector, especially NRC, became rather used to initiating scientific programs suggested more and more frequently by "in-house" judgments about what constituted appropriate priorities. This was perfectly justified in the wartime environment of secrecy and urgency. There is a real sense, however, in which these wartime habits became difficult to change in the post-war environment, such that the government science sector tended, in *relative terms*, to make less real use of the advisory committees and other machinery which they had consciously created in the earlier periods to link themselves with their scientist colleagues in the non-governmental science community. *Vis-à-vis* their scientist colleagues outside the government, government scientists, especially at NRC, enjoyed a position of greater power and status.

## (c) The Glassco Commission

With respect to the scientists' relationships with politicians, the 1950's appear to have been a period where science was viewed by politicians with some awe and mystery.[8] To a degree more noticeable than at perhaps any other period in Canada's history, the science budget appeared to be granted "on faith". This was not equally true for all agencies in the federal government but the tendency for politicians and scientists to live at a kind of arms-length relationship with one another was strong.

---

6 NRC, *Annual Report, 1945-1946*, p. 10.

7 For a brief account of the Howe-Mackenzie relationship see J. Porter, *The Vertical Mosaic* (Toronto, University of Toronto Press, 1965), pp. 430-32. The high regard of the scientists in the federal bureaucracy for Mr. Howe was clearly impressed upon the writer in the course of several interviews.

8 See House of Commons, *Special Committee on the Operations of the National Research Council, Minutes of Proceedings* (Ottawa, King's Printer, 1950). See also *Debates* (Commons) (April 18, 1950), p. 1,679.

The strength of this development was revealed when the Glassco Commission on Government Organization reported in 1963 with a very critical judgment of the Government's science policy machinery.

Commenting on the Privy Council Committee, the NRC, and the Advisory Panel for Scientific Policy (an inter-departmental committee of deputy ministers created in 1949) the Glassco study charged that

> the system has failed to function as intended. The Privy Council Committee has met infrequently, and between 1950 and 1958 was not called together at all. The National Research Council has turned aside from its original duty of advising on broad national policy and has concentrated its efforts, albeit with conspicuous success, on the support of research and scholarships in the universities and, in a general way, on its own laboratories and establishments and the fields of science in which they operate. The Advisory panel met formally fourteen times in its first ten years of existence and has since convened only infrequently.[9]

As a result the Commission felt that decisions about science tended to fall by default to the Treasury Board and its staff, a group which had minimal technical competence in *this* field, and decisions tended, therefore, to be based on which ministers could wield the greatest power.

To rationalize the input of science and scientists into governmental decision-making, the Glassco Commission recommended that a "central scientific bureau" be created to act as a science secretariat to the Cabinet. It also recommended that a "National Scientific Advisory Council" be established, a structure which was to be broadly representative of the scientific disciplines and of the university, industrial and governmental sectors. The central bureau would serve the Advisory Council and the bureau's head officer would be the secretary of the Council. The Commission rejected the concept of a Department of Science and suggested that the Bureau's head would report to the President of the Treasury Board. The object was to avoid the difficulties of NRC which had the difficult role of trying to be an objective advisor in addition to promoting the vested interests of its own laboratories in competition with other science based departments.[10]

In 1964, following the receipt of a further personal study by Dr. C. J. Mackenzie,[11] the Pearson Government took steps to create the necessary science policy machinery. In April of 1964 it announced the formation

[9] *Royal Commission on Government Organization* (Ottawa, Queen's Printer), Vol. 4, Special Areas of Administration, Report No. 23, *Scientific and Industrial Research*, p. 220.
[10] *Ibid.*, pp. 220-24.
[11] C. J. Mackenzie, *Report to Prime Minister on Government Science* (Ottawa, Queen's Printer, 1964).

of the bureau to be called the Science Secretariat and in 1966 legislation was passed creating the Science Council of Canada which was the name ultimately given to the advisory council.[12] The fact that the two parts of the machinery were created two years apart has had important consequences not only for the scientist-politician relationship but also for the relationship *among* scientists and science agencies in the governmental bureaucracy. Much of the debate in the 1966 to 1969 period has centred, apart from the substantive outputs of policy, on the problems generated on the "input" side by the initial vagueness in the central machinery. Several consequences can be briefly stated:

First, other agencies (especially the NRC which in 1964, by statute, retained its advisory role) were extremely uncertain about what kind of power the secretariat might have over their affairs, an uncertainty by no means resolved by the government's official assertion that the structure would be a "small fact-finding and analytical group serving in a staff capacity without executive authority".[13] In this respect the scientists in the several agencies viewed the Science Secretariat in much the same way that the rest of the bureaucracy views the Treasury Board – that is, with a healthy suspicion.

A second consequence that developed was that by the time the Science Council was created in 1966 the Science Secretariat had launched itself into a program of studies for the Privy Council Office and had little time to serve the Science Council when the latter began to launch its own program of long-range studies. Difficulties also arose because of the fact that the Science Secretariat was a *confidential* advisor to the Cabinet and the Science Council was designed to be an *open* structure designed partly to generate public debate about science policy. It became exceedingly difficult for the Science Secretariat to divide its time and work priorities between two masters.[14] This structural ambivalence was corrected by the recent separation of the two bodies, the Science Council to be entirely independent with its own staff and the Science Secretariat to retain its role as confidential advisor.[15] The prospect, therefore, is that the internal machinery (the Science Secretariat) will be shortly joined by a "competitive" outside structure (the Science Council) which in all likelihood will find it necessary to build up a considerable staff of its own.

---

12 See *Debates* (Commons) (April 30, 1964), p. 2,752, and (March 17, 1966), pp. 2,848-53, for statements and debates on the Science Secretariat and Science Council respectively.

13 *Debates* (Commons) (April 30, 1964), p. 2,752.

14 The ambivalence of the relationship was revealed before a Senate Committee recently. See *Senate, Special Committee on Science Policy, Proceedings*, Phase 1 (Ottawa, Queen's Printer, 1968), pp. 127-50.

15 *Debates* (Commons) (February 27, 1969), pp. 6,016-17.

In the light of the changes in machinery it becomes exceedingly hazardous to assess the relative degree of influence that scientists may now have in the federal government and bureaucracy. There are certainly larger numbers of scientists located in or near the central structures of government, but this in itself does not guarantee an enhanced position for the scientist as advisor.

The ultimate judgments that can be made about the position of scientists in the Canadian bureaucracy and governmental structure will be based on the kinds of science programs and outputs that emerge, rather than on the machinery itself. On this score it is also difficult to make confident judgments, especially in the light of the recent cancellation of two multi-million dollar projects, the Intense Neutron Generator ($150 million) and the Queen Elizabeth II Telescope ($25 million).[16] Both were projects initiated by government agencies before and during the periods of "machinery" adjustment described above. They have been the object of much discussion and have frequently been used as indications of the lack of a real science policy and of adequate science policy machinery. They have also been cited as evidence that scientists (in spite of the politicians' recent "talk" about the importance of science) still have insufficient influence in political circles.[17]

These decisions, however, do not constitute the total output or response in the past three years. The government has made decisions giving approval to a $20 million research facility called TRIUMF,[18] to significantly increased expenditures on industrial research programs,[19] to an oceanographic expedition,[20] and to a fresh water research institute.[21] It has also given significant research emphasis to the recently created Department of Communications.[22]

When science "outputs" of this kind are added it suggests that the advice of *some* scientists both inside and outside of the government is being heeded, or at least that their advice coincides with some of the priority preferences of the political sector. It suggests that any judgments

---

[16] See *Science Forum* (February, 1968); *The Globe and Mail* (August 30, 1968), p. 1, and (September 18, 1968), p. 20.

[17] See, for example, an editorial in *The Globe and Mail* (March 4, 1969), p. 6 and *Debates* (Commons) (March 10, 1969), pp. 6,445-46.

[18] See *Senate, Special Committee on Science Policy, Proceedings* (November 20, 1968), pp. 1,044-45.

[19] For a survey of the increased emphasis on industrial programs see *Ottawa Citizen* (February 5, 1969), p. 18.

[20] *Debates* (Commons) (January 16, 1969), p. 4,355.

[21] See Science Secretariat, Special Study No. 5, *Water Resources Research in Canada* (Ottawa, Queen's Printer, 1968), pp. 35-37.

[22] *Debates* (Commons) (February 28, 1969), pp. 6,078-79.

we might wish to make about the relative influence of scientists must consider not only the views of scientists whose advice has been recently rejected but *also* the views of scientists whose advice has been recently accepted. To this extent at least the position of the scientist as advisor seems strangely familiar and parallel to other kinds of experts.

There is general agreement that an increased proportion of our national expenditure must be spent on science and on research and development and that our governmental-bureaucratic machinery must permit us to make these allocations intelligently. There seems to be less realization, however, that intragovernmental "politics" by which these decisions are made depends as much on the political relations *between scientists* and science agencies as it does on the political relations between the scientist and the politician.

# 16 Pressure-Group Activity and Policy Formation: Collective Bargaining in the Federal Public Service*

## Robert Armstrong

When the Public Service Staff Relations Act received Royal Assent on February 23, 1967, it signalled an end to ten years of development, adaptation and change in employer-employee relations in the federal public service. The purpose of this paper is not to provide an analysis of the legislation nor primarily a history of staff relations. It is rather an attempt to track the long and difficult policy trail leading to the achievement of collective bargaining. It is an attempt also to probe the changes of attitude and values and the shifts of power that took place within a period of approximately ten years and which made the passage of Bill C-170 seem finally like a very normal occurrence.

In December, 1958, the Civil Service Commission issued a report on personnel administration in the public service which was a review of civil service legislation. The basic policy issue posed by the Report and by the bills based upon it, subsequently introduced into Parliament, was to what extent and how employees would participate in the determination of their pay and working conditions. The commissioners "concluded that the differences in the circumstances of private and public employment do

* Robert Armstrong, "Some Aspects of Policy Determination in the Development of the Collective Bargaining Legislation in the Public Service of Canada," *Canadian Public Administration*, Vol. 11, No. 4 (Winter, 1968), pp. 485-93 (reprinted and abridged by permission of author and publisher).

not readily admit of the simple and unqualified application to the Civil Service of the normal industrial pattern of collective bargaining."[1]

The Commission's solution was set out in Appendix "B" of the Report with disarming simplicity.[2] In it the Commission would provide the auspices under which representatives of the employer and representatives of the organized staff associations would discuss questions of salary and wages. The plan was that the Commission would provide a chairman "who would be responsible for the proper conduct of the discussions." The discussions would take place before the Commission's recommendations to government on any particular issue were made. These recommendations would be communicated simultaneously to the government and the staff associations. Final decision on the recommendations would remain a matter for the government.

The basis of the Appendix "B" solution was the commissioners' appreciation of the Commission's independent status on matters of pay and conditions of work. It was not subject to outside pressures, the Report said. Its responsibility was to make recommendations to government based on objective examination and analysis. That the Commission was independent and that its recommendations were indeed its own cannot be challenged. However, the proposal did not provide for true bilateral negotiations. A further weakness of the proposal and one of the main reasons for its rejection by organized employees was that, while the Commission recommendations were independently based and might as such have commended themselves to the government, the assertion that "the government acts upon the recommendations which the Commission puts forward"[3] was an accurate description of the relationship only up to the time of the Report. In 1959, the government rejected a Commission pay recommendation.

In 1961, the Government introduced Bill C-71, an Act respecting the Civil Service of Canada. For the employee organizations as for the Government the paramount issue in Bill C-71 was employee participation in the establishment of rates of pay and other conditions of work.

In their appearances before the House of Commons Special Committee on the Civil Service Act to which Bill C-71 was referred, the employee organizations were cautious and somewhat tentative in their proposals. Most of them wanted direct negotiations with the Government. Eschewing the strike, they were in favour of settling disputes by arbitration. The

---

[1] Civil Service Commission, *Personnel Administration in the Public Service* (Ottawa, Queen's Printer, 1958), p. 14.

[2] *Ibid.*, p. 132-33.

[3] *Ibid.*, paragraph 60, p. 23.

Canadian Postal Employees' Association was an exception; it wanted to be brought within the scope of the Industrial Relations and Disputes Investigation Act. It wanted collective bargaining and the right to strike. In 1961, the Postal Employees were an affiliate of the then Civil Service Federation of Canada, the largest of the civil service organizations. The Federation was strongly in favour of direct negotiation and arbitration on the United Kingdom model. It is doubtful that the Federation executive realized how damaging it would be to its own case to have an affiliated organization taking a position so opposite to its own on this basic issue.

The employee organizations, or staff associations as they were then generally known, had not really thought through the implications of full-blown collective bargaining and it was not what most of them then wanted. Their proposals were not couched in the language of labour relations. In addition, Bill C-71 did not help them focus on the technical and structural side of bargaining for the simple reason that it was a Civil Service Act primarily concerned with the merit principle and not a labour relations statute. The Canadian Labour Congress alone recognized that because of the considerable diversity of organization among employee associations there would have to be some formalized procedures for recognition.[4] The Congress then proceeded to offer a sophisticated outline of the "two principal devices available to labour and management for the settlement of disputes; the strike (or lockout) and the arbitration board."[5] The Congress's own preference was for the strike.

The Government's view, which was expressed by Mr. Fleming, then Minister of Finance, and backed by the largest majority in Canadian parliamentary history, was that there should be no resort to radical or untried forms of legislation. The Government's position was that there had to be an advance based on precedent and experience and that the consultation procedure provided for in the Bill was an appropriate vehicle for employee representations at that time. There would be no arbitration. There would be no collective bargaining. In addition, Mr. Fleming pointed out "that the views of the staff associations themselves on matters of representation fall somewhat short of unanimity."[6]

The Civil Service Act which received Royal Assent on September 29, 1961, provided for consultation, of which Claude Jodoin, President of the Canadian Labour Congress, said: "However much they may be consult-

---

4 Minutes of Proceedings and Evidence, House of Commons, Special Committee on the Civil Service Act, 1961, No. 6, p. 137.

5 *Ibid.*, p. 139.

6 *Ibid.*, No. 23, p. 537.

ed, the staff associations and the trade unions which represent government employees will under this legislation remain what they were before, essentially supplicants."[7] For the employee organizations, the continuing flaw in consultation was that, consult for as long as they might, it was the Government employer which finally set the rates of pay and conditions of service. Government officials were not enamoured with the process either. It was a situation, they said, where the employee organizations consulted before and complained after.

Prior to the 1963 general election, the President of the Civil Service Federation of Canada, Mr. C. A. Edwards, took what proved to be a decisive step. He wrote to Prime Minister Diefenbaker, the Leader of the Opposition, Mr. Pearson, the Leader of the New Democratic Party, Mr. Douglas, and the National Leader of the Social Credit Party, Mr. Thompson, asking each for the official position of his party on the questions of the principle of negotiation and arbitration for the civil service and the specific proposals of the Civil Service Federation for a negotiation procedure in the civil service.[8] Mr. Diefenbaker replied that he and his colleagues "having noted that the Federation and other Civil Service Associations do not claim the right to strike, the Government fully endorses acceptance of the principle of collective bargaining."[9] Mr. Pearson quoted a resolution adopted by the National Council of the National Liberal Federation of Canada in 1962 that the "Liberal Party believes that the Civil Service should be granted the right to joint negotiations and arbitration, while at the same time recognizing that the supremacy of Parliament means that the right to strike cannot be granted."[10] As for the machinery required to give effect to the resolution, Mr. Pearson said that a Liberal government would set it up "only after the most careful consideration by the government and the fullest consultation with representatives of the Civil Service."[11]

After the election, the new Government moved very quickly to honour the commitment the party had made while in opposition. On August 7, 1963, Prime Minister Pearson announced the appointment of a special committee of senior officials to make the necessary preparations for the establishment in the public service of an appropriate form of collective

---

[7] *Ibid.*, p. 132.

[8] Civil Service Federation News Letter (April, 1963).

[9] *Ibid.* Positive responses were received from all leaders. Speaking for his party, Mr. Douglas said that "the Government of Canada should stand in the same relationship to its employees as all other employers."

[10] *Ibid.*

[11] *Ibid.*

bargaining and arbitration. The committee, which was known as the Preparatory Committee on Collective Bargaining in the Public Service, was under the chairmanship of Mr. A. D. P. Heeney, and was to make recommendations to the Cabinet. The Committee was supported by a staff drawn from both inside and outside the public service. It received representations from and had discussions with the representatives of a number of employee organizations and central labour bodies. The staff put together in the early months a series of studies that surveyed past and present patterns of staff and industrial relations in the various Canadian jurisdictions and in other countries.

As a policy advising body, the Preparatory Committee was a unique device. It was not a royal commission and for that reason its relationship to the Government was a good deal less formal. In its Report of July, 1965, the Committee stated that in May of 1964 it had "communicated to the Cabinet its proposals for reforms in the systems of classification and pay and the broad outline of a plan for collective bargaining and arbitration in the Public Service."[12] On the resolution stage of the Collective Bargaining Bill, the Prime Minister said that after the report of the Committee was received and published, "the chairman and other members of the Committee and its staff continued to assist ministers."[13] There seems little doubt that early in its proceedings the Preparatory Committee established what must have become a continuing liaison with ministers.

A committee of cabinet was established to consider and report on the policy issues identified by the Preparatory Committee and to weigh its proposals. Because of the make-up of the Preparatory Committee, it was difficult for employee organizations not to take the view that its recommendations tended to favour the employer. This was not an unreasonable position and some government officials recognized the liability. Had a royal commission been charged with the task set for the Preparatory Committee, this feeling might have been lessened. But it is doubtful that the senior officials who composed the Committee could have been completely insulated from advising the Government on such complex policy matters which would have such fundamental consequences for administration or that the Government would or could have deprived itself of their advice. The Preparatory Committee device appears to have been an effective way of devising policy in an area where the Government was necessarily an interested party. In addition, there is some doubt that

---

[12] Preparatory Committee on Collective Bargaining in the Public Service (Ottawa, Queen's Printer, 1965), p. 2.
[13] *Debates* (Commons) (April 25, 1966), p. 4,243.

an outside body would have had sufficient momentum to set in motion the sweeping administrative changes that attended the introduction of collective bargaining.

The reaction of employee organizations to the Report of the Preparatory Committee was mixed. Organizations were pleased that collective bargaining was a step nearer; but there were reservations. The major organization, the Civil Service Federation, was disappointed that the proposed Public Service Staff Relations Act did not provide for a formal relationship at the departmental level and felt that its existence as a federation of departmental organizations was threatened by the provisions which based bargaining units on the emerging horizontal and service-wide occupational groups. The postal unions, as they were to demonstrate shortly, would not accept a dispute settlement process which ended in arbitration. No one was happy with the provision that would have given the Governor in Council the power to "amend, set aside, or suspend until a specified future date, the operation of the whole or any part of the (arbitral) award."[14] This provision did not appear in the Bill.

During the summer of 1965 and even before the Preparatory Committee had reported, representatives of the Civil Service Federation of Canada and the Civil Service Association of Canada were engaged in a series of increasingly crucial meetings aimed at welding the two associations into one new disciplined organization. The Public Service Alliance was formally established early in the fall of 1966. The merger had taken place between the time the Public Service Staff Relations Act had been referred to a Special Joint Committee of the Senate and of the House of Commons and the time the Committee had reported. At the beginning of the Committee's hearings, the two associations appeared separately and put in separate briefs which were later consolidated with the leave of the Committee.

By its terms of reference, the Preparatory Committee was to recommend an appropriate form of collective bargaining and arbitration. The cornerstone of its recommendations, therefore, rested on arbitration as the method of dispute settlement. It reported that it had considered the possibility of proposing that strike action be prohibited in the statute establishing the system of collective bargaining but it decided not to recommend a statutory prohibition. "Looking at the recent history of the Public Service," they "concluded that it would be difficult to justify a prohibition on grounds of demonstrated need."[15] Within a few weeks

---

[14] Preparatory Committee on Collective Bargaining in the Public Service, *op. cit.*, sec. 60.
[15] *Ibid.*, p. 36.

of the Report being made public, the postal workers went on strike to support demands for higher wages and better working conditions. The strike demonstrated a number of things. A strike of public servants could take place. A strike of public servants could have a measure of public support, if it seemed justified. A strike of public servants was not necessarily a national calamity. In the light of what was for many people a successful strike of public servants, the government varied the recommendations of the Preparatory Committee in drafting the Bill. When Bill C-170 was introduced into the House of Commons, it contained two methods of dispute settlement. Bargaining agents would have a choice between arbitration or strike action. Strike action would be restricted to some degree but the principle itself was enunciated very clearly. Speaking to the resolution on which Bill C-170 was based, the Prime Minister pointed out that most public servants represented by the various organizations wanted to be governed by arbitration but that "many other responsible Canadians also feel strongly that the right to strike is fundamental and should be qualified only where a clear case can be made to restrict that right in the public interest. The government believes that these strong and very genuine feelings should be respected."[16]

The Bill which was introduced into the House of Commons on April 25, 1966, though generous in its concepts and principles and on the whole well received by employee organizations, was cautious in its detail and tended to rigidity by attempting to anticipate all possible contingencies. In addition, the charge could be made that "the government, in anticipation of its role as employer has arranged the rules of the game to suit itself."[17] Ministers and officials may indeed have resolved issues in favour of the employer but the Government appeared willing to overcome any suggestion of bias. The Prime Minister made it clear that the Government was prepared to consider suggestions for change and to support those which could improve the Bill. Working in a non-partisan atmosphere, the Special Committee made many improvements. All its proposed amendments were accepted by the Government. The Act was proclaimed in force on March 13, 1967, and the first applications for certification were made on April 13, 1967. Bargaining agents were certified and negotiations begun but a considerable time necessarily elapsed before the first agreement was signed.

In retrospect, the enactment of a law establishing collective bargaining in the public service of Canada may well appear a normal and even necessary event – something that was inevitable. Clearly, however, the

---

16 *Debates* (Commons) (April 25, 1966), p. 4,246.
17 Brief of the Canadian Labour Congress to the Joint Committee, p. 18.

statute was not the result of one straight, sustained line of development. That the legislation was enacted in 1967 was more the result of a number of variable factors acting and interacting at particular times. Some of the lines of force had been developing for some time and may have been plotted with some accuracy but there were other newer forces which could not have been foreseen.

In 1961, the Associations were rebuffed. The majority of them had asked for direct negotiation and arbitration. There had been a consensus growing around the idea of an arbitration tribunal on the United Kingdom model but the associations did not mobilize that consensus. They were in a political setting but they seemed unable to engage in the political process.[18] There was considerable fear of being tagged partisan. Whatever leverage they may have had was lost when most of them declared that they would not strike. In 1963, the associations demonstrated growing sophistication. They found that political action could be a neutral instrument. Mr. Edward's letter was the most dramatic expression of this new sophistication. Internally, efforts to unite the associations into a broad working group and some of them into an organic whole proceeded. The organic unity of the two largest associations was achieved in 1966. The associations quickly learned that if in unity there could be diversity there could also be considerable strength. Their major achievement in five years was to mobilize that strength and to have it respected by the Government.

In 1961, the Government had an enormous majority. Only a minority of the organized employees sought the right to strike and collective bargaining under the Industrial Relations and Disputes Investigation Act. However, the minority fared no better than the majority who wanted arbitration. In 1967, the minority Liberal Government was careful to work out a consensus and to respect the legitimate interests of both the majority and the minority.

It is not at all certain that the legislation would have provided for the right to strike if there had not been a strike of postal workers in 1965. At one stroke, the strike was a fact. It could be cribbed and confined but no longer could it be said that it could not happen. Attention was turned to a question of practical significance. If a strike does take place, how do you ensure the continuance of vital services? The legislation attempts to provide the necessary safeguards. Without the strike in the summer of 1965, the Bill passed in 1967 may not have provided for this alternative method of dispute settlement. What finally shaped Bill C-170 was the

---

18 That the Government itself demonstrated a lack of political skill is also true, particularly if politics is seen as an activity by which differing interests are conciliated: cf. Bernard Crick, *In Defence of Politics.*

Special Joint Committee of the Senate and of the House of Commons. That the Committee would have brought together men and women of such wide experience could not have been foreseen. Their work improved the Bill significantly. It can be said of the Committee, if we may paraphrase Edmund Burke, that it worked in the interest of one constituency – Canada.

# 17 New Centres of Policy-Making Influence*

## Maurice Lamontagne

I shall devote my remarks mainly to the influence being felt by the politician, particularly by ministers since they are the most important and the most successful politicians. But first, let us see how the rise and fall of ministers came about. To describe this most interesting evolution, I wish to rely on an article published by the *Economist* in 1947 and entitled "The Twilight of Ministers." Those of you who have already read that article will undoubtedly remember its opening paragraph:

> The principle of complete royal subjection to ministerial control was firmly embedded in the British Constitution in the course of the nineteenth century. Though theoretically all powerful the Monarch had, by the end of Queen Victoria's reign, completely accepted the position that he could do nothing without ministerial advice and, indeed, that he could not refuse to do anything that his Ministers advised him to do.

In Canada, a similar evolution took place at about the same time. It started in 1791 and reached a very important moment in 1848 when the principle of responsible government was recognized. The Byng incident in 1926 merely served to formalize what was already implicit. But this rise of ministers to a position of great influence was not to last very long.

The correspondent of the *Economist* goes on to say:

* Maurice Lamontagne, "The Influence of the Politician," *Canadian Public Administration*, Vol. 11, No. 3 (Fall, 1968), pp. 263-71 (reprinted and slightly abridged by permission of author and publisher).

But there is no such thing as finality in human development. The cabinet had no sooner removed the last formal checks on its power than it, too, began to be something of an outward show and the reality of power began to move elsewhere. Ministers, in the middle of the twentieth century, were subject to three pressures which together made it impossible for them to fulfil the role that the Constitution, as then understood, assigned to them. In the first place, with the advent of Socialism, the subject-matter of state action was enormously extended. Secondly, the subject-matter of public affairs became much more technical and difficult and this, coinciding with the growth of the belief that it was a positive advantage for a politician to have spent his formative years in the mine or at the bench, made it a rarity for a Minister to be able to understand the papers that were put before him, even if he had time to read them. Thirdly, the number of personal appearances required of a Minister – in Parliament, at conferences, and at luncheons, dinners and meetings of all kinds – increased so greatly that even these activities, hitherto pre-eminently those of the Minister himself, came to be beyond the powers of a single man, except with the assistance of a Public Relations officer. Under these pressures, the Minister gradually became a figure-head . . . only those Ministers who combined the most forceful personalities with a willingness to work cruelly long hours could really be said to be responsible for their own words and actions, let alone those of the Department they nominally controlled.

But this gradual change was not apparent for many years. The permanent civil servants, while engrossing more and more of the reality of power, studiously preserved the outward forms of Ministerial supremacy – as, indeed, Ministers in their turn did [as regards] the King. Just as laws were still enacted "by the King's Most Excellent Majesty", and Ministers spoke of their "loyal duty" to the Crown, so also the most eminent and powerful civil servant would still refer to his Minister as "my master", and would begin his letters, "I am directed by the Secretary of State . . .".

This long quotation sums up very well also what happened in Canada. I need here to recall just a few landmarks which illustrate the fall of ministers and the rise of civil servants. The civil service began to emerge as a new force with the recognition of the merit system and the creation of the Civil Service Commission in 1917. Fifty years later, the peak of its rise was reached when, a few months ago, full bargaining rights were granted by Parliament to the staff associations. Some objections were raised before the adoption of this important piece of legislation. Her Majesty the Queen could not bargain with her subjects. The supremacy of Parliament could not be encroached upon by collective agreements. The fact that these arguments were not even considered seriously shows how removed our political symbolism has become from the new reality.

Meanwhile, especially after 1935, the Establishment emerged and gradually became the centre of power within the federal administration. Generally speaking, at least until recently, when the Establishment was united behind or against a certain policy, its advice was accepted by the Cabinet; when there was a division of opinion between the officials of a particular department and those of the Department of Finance, including the Treasury Board, then the views of the latter would prevail at the Cabinet table. I have seen situations when two important groups of the Establishment had not been able to reconcile their views on vital policy issues; in those circumstances, the Cabinet failed to act.

The supremacy of the Establishment may have reached its peak recently when, as a result of the implementation of the Glassco report, deputy ministers have been given important managerial responsibilities which had been viewed before as being too sensitive to be exercised by ministers and had been transferred to the Civil Service Commission. The special position of influence of the Establishment was underlined again not long ago when a minister was asked to resign by the Opposition for having consulted outside experts and when another minister had to resign for having reached a decision without proper consultation with his civil servants.

A story, which is supposed to be true, illustrates the fall of ministers and the rise of civil servants. It is reported that a Liberal backbencher who had ambitions and also a sense of humour decided one day to write to Mr. King and ask to be appointed to the Cabinet. In his reply, Mr. King, who could then afford to be straightforward, told the daring backbencher that he did not have the competence and the high intellectual qualifications required for such an important assignment. The persistent member, who was obviously not satisfied with this answer, wrote back to Mr. King and said: "My dear Prime Minister, I believe that you have misunderstood the nature of my request; high as my ambition can aspire, I do not expect to become a deputy minister, I merely want to be a minister!" Whether it is true or not, this story symbolizes very succinctly "the twilight of ministers" in Canada.

Nous ne devrions pas conclure, cependant, que le pouvoir des hauts fonctionnaires s'est toujours manifesté dans le même sens et qu'il n'a jamais connu de limites. A mon avis, l'apogée de leur influence positive coincida avec les dernières années du régime St Laurent. Sous l'administration Diefenbaker, leur rôle fut surtout négatif selon le témoignage souvent répété de l'honorable Alvin Hamilton. A l'en croire, les projets du gouvernement conservateur étaient systématiquement bloqués par les hauts fonctionnaires. Cet aveu en dit long sur l'impuissance des ministres de cette périod. Par contre, au cours des fameux 60 premiers jours du gouvernement Pearson, l'influence des hauts fonctionnaires fut presque nulle. Cette indépendance retrouvée conduisit à des erreurs qui ne seront pas facilement oubliées et le déséquilibre traditionnel des forces en présence fut rapidement rétabli.

J'ai la conviction, toutefois, que nous franchissons déjà les premières étapes d'une nouvelle période. Le parti libéral, dans l'opposition et avec l'aide de conseillers qui n'appartennient évidemment pas à la fonction publique, avait préparé un programme précis et détaillé. L'erreur qui fut faite en arrivant au pouvoir de le mettre à exécution trop rapidement et dans l'isolement n'aura d'importance à long terme. Seule en aura le méthode suivie par les libéraux dans l'élaboration de leur programme et qui s'inspirait d'ailleurs de celle que l'équipe de Jean Lesage avait utilisée avant 1960. J'ai l'impression que l'expérience faite par le parti libéral dans l'opposition sera dorénavant répétée par tous les principaux partis politiques, même ceux qui sont parvenus au pouvoir. C'est là l'un des facteurs qui me portent à croire qu'une ère nouvelle quant aux sources de l'influence politique est déjà commencée au Canada.

Thus, a new period is emerging in our country. I would describe it as the "twilight of civil servants." I do not mean by this that the fall of the civil servant will be as dramatic as that of the politician many years ago or that it will correspond to the rise of ministers to a new position of influence. I mean, however, that the Establishment will play a more limited role than in the past 25 years and that it will have to share its privileged position near ministers with new sources of political influence.

In the first place, I believe that civil servants will have less and less to do with the development of new policies. Conversely, the intellectual community outside the civil service will play an increasing role in the determination of new policy objectives and proposals. The rising number of royal commissions, task forces, advisory boards, and councils is an obvious sign of the shift which is taking place. But it is only part of the new story.

In the past, political parties could win elections by making vague promises, by relying on their record, or merely by attacking the opposition. When they assumed office, they were not committed to an over-all political program and they were free to accept the advice of civil servants even in connection with the formulation of policy. This situation is changing rapidly. The public and the press now expect political parties to be identified with a concrete, detailed, and co-ordinated set of policy proposals, especially during electoral campaigns. Moreover, this identification has become almost inevitable since political parties have decided to hold national conventions every two years. Their public image would greatly suffer if such meetings were not devoted to serious thinking and discussion. But such an identification means that when a given party is newly elected or even is returned to office, it will be committed to a detailed set of policies which will have been developed with little, if any, consultation with civil servants.

The politician, however, will not be more responsible for the formulation of policy than he was before. But he will have new masters. The new pattern for the preparation of political platforms is already set. It involves the consultation of the public by taking polls and conducting motivation surveys in order to know the priorities of its needs and preoccupations and also, more and more frequently, the calling of a thinkers' conference to determine how those priorities can best be met. Resolutions based on this preliminary work will then be adopted in a more or less modified form by national conventions and become the official platform of our political parties. Thus, the public without really knowing it and the intellectual community will become new sources of political influence and will play an increasing role in the selection and the formulation of policies.

There is another new pattern which is emerging and which will tend also to reduce the influence of civil servants while not contributing to increase the importance of ministers. It has to do with the working of Parliament. In the immediate past, Parliament had really very little to do with legislation. The legislative program originated mainly from the Establishment which also prepared the ministerial speeches required for its presentation to the House of Commons. It was expected that once a bill had been accepted by Cabinet on the advice of the Establishment it would also be approved without modification by Parliament. In the House of Commons, the opposition could speak as long as it wished but it would have been a great sign of weakness on the part of a minister to accept any of its suggestions. As to the government backbenchers, they were expected to be seen when votes were called but not to be heard.

That situation is changing rapidly. We can even speak of a quiet revolution in Parliament. The private member, after having lost his administrative influence, which is a disguised definition of patronage, is now acquiring a legislative role which he should have had all along.

Several factors account for this change: the improvement in the quality of members, the succession of minority governments, and the length of sessions. It is fair to say that the evolution really originated from the government side. Competent backbenchers became tired of having to sit in the House with very little to do. They began to present their grievances at party caucuses and to press for more and better organized parliamentary committees. Ministers were not in a very good position to resist those pressures. It is indeed interesting to note that, with the minority situation and the length of sessions, ministers have never been more exposed to the influence of their own backbenchers. This is even more so when they have long-term political ambitions. In certain cases, it is not an exaggeration to say that they meet private members more often than their own officials. As a result, parliamentary committees have never been more influential than during the present sessions. They have proposed new legislation which the government will have to bring forward and they have substantially modified several important bills. Such an intrusion of Parliament in the legislative process would not have been tolerated just a few years ago.

Parliamentary reform has been long overdue. It has now become inevitable. When it comes, you will see that a lot of frivolities which the House of Commons is now engaged in will be removed, that Parliament will be more interested in the substance and less in the detail of legislative proposals, and that greater emphasis will be placed on parliamentary committees.

We are moving towards a compromise between the British and the American political institutions. As we reach it, the influence of civil servants in the legislative process will be less important. At least one type of politician will become more influential since the legislative role of the private member will be expanding.

Finally, I would like to mention a third and undoubtedly the most important new force which is competing with civil servants to influence ministers. I mean the press, broadly speaking, or the so-called mass media. If the correspondent of the *Economist* quoted at the beginning of my remarks is right when he says that the Cabinet has become "something of an outward show," then the main objective of a minister who wants to be successful and remain in the show ought to be to develop and maintain a good public image. Save the surface and you save all. Hence, the growing importance for a minister to be friendly with reporters and to have an efficient executive assistant or public relations officer.

Here again, substantial changes have taken place. In the past, the relationship between ministers and the means of communication was quite different. Television and even radio did not establish themselves as influential image-makers before the mid 50's. The press had a partisan approach to politics. Its owners, generally speaking, were closely identified with a political party and they made sure that their newspapers and their reporters would faithfully reflect their political views. In that context, the public image of the politician was largely determined by the good or bad relationship which existed between himself or, more precisely, his political party and individual publishers. Once that relationship had been defined, ministers could do very little about their image, especially on a day-to-day basis. It was not, therefore, one of their main daily preoccupations.

The philosophy of the mass media has changed drastically in the last decades. They have become businesses, and competition among them is acute. Party affiliation has disappeared or barely survives in the editorial page. The number of readers or audience rating has become the golden rule. In addition, there is the cynical assumption that the public has a strong preference for sensation.

This approach leads to a new role of ethics for reporters. From now on, they do not have to reflect the political views of their employers; thus, they can transmit their own in their articles. The thing they cannot afford is to be dull. But straight and objective information is not supposed to be interesting. So, the reporter who wants to be successful looks for rumours, scoops, and leaks. He writes today on the news of tomorrow. He puts the emphasis on personalities rather than on events. He appraises rather than informs. He is interested in the surface rather than in performance. He has few real friends but he is grateful to those who enable him to produce his daily article or his news broadcast "every hour on the hour". In previous days, he used to work hard to find an official source for his information; nowadays it is easier for him to rely on Cabinet leaks originating from ministers' offices.

Je ne crois pas avoir grandement caricaturé la réalité. J'ai vu des ministres portés aux nues par les journalistes avant même qu'ils aient pu faire quoi que ce soit et se faire détruire ensuite pour s'être montrés tout simplement humains. J'ai connu des ministres qui continuaient à avoir une bonne presse sans rien accomplir de valable. J'ai enfin entendu des journalistes me dire qu'ils avaient laissé la profession parce que, pendant le période des soi-disant scandales, ils avaient l'impression tous les soirs d'avoir du sang jusqu'aux coudes.

This general situation was always tempered by noble exceptions and has improved recently. It remains, however, that the minister who is preoccupied by his public image, as projected by the mass media, faces a difficult challenge. But, if he is not worried by it, he cannot continue for long to be a successful politician. There is, here, a paradoxical situation which I would like to explore more fully.

My contention is – and I could substantiate it by an impressive set of facts – that the mass media do not have a decisive impact on public opinion, at least in so far as politics is concerned. It would take too long for me to outline the factors which account for this situation. I will add, however, that most politicians share my view and recognize, in theory, that the mass media do not effectively guide or faithfully reflect public opinion. Ministers could, therefore, afford to ignore them, at least up to a point. Some successful politicians have done just that. In fact, however, most politicians are "newsworms". They are as fond of rumours, scoops, and personal stories as most reporters. Both groups live in the same isolated world, although they usually despise each other. This cohabitation produces strange results. In most cases, the politician is almost unconsciously mystified by the reporter. Thus, while the mass media have little impact on the public, they have a great deal of influence on the politician. There lies the secret of the rising power of the press. It is in this restricted context that a minister cannot ignore the mass media with impunity. If he enjoys a good press, he will be envied and respected or feared by his colleagues. If he has no press, he has no future. And, if he has a bad press, he is in serious trouble, because he will be viewed even by his own associates as a political liability, in spite of the qualities he may have.

That is why it has become almost essential for a successful minister to have a dual personality, to smile even if he does not feel like it, to talk when he should remain silent, to say the "right" thing in spite of his own convictions. That is why also ministers have two ears; one for the press and one for their policy advisers. What they hear from both ears may often be incompatible. The danger is that the desire to preserve the public image may prevail over the requirements of the public interest. In any case, it should be obvious by now that civil servants must be prepared to share with the press the monopolistic influence they used to have on ministers. From now on, ministers have to live in the limelight. This new position also contributes to the twilight of civil servants.

My general thesis can be summed up very briefly. To begin with, I make the distinction between the symbol of power and the reality of power or the real source of political influence. Then I contend that we have gone through different phases of a long evolution. It started with absolute monarchy which coincided, broadly speaking, with the colonial period. Then, with the development of our democratic institutions and the granting of responsible government, the Cabinet was recognized as the supreme political authority. Since World War II, gradually and for a variety of reasons, the Civil Service Establishment became identified with the reality of power. Although ministers could still do wrong and continued to be held responsible for their departments, they merely represented, in most cases, the authentic symbol of power. As to the Monarch, he could do no wrong and therefore could do nothing. He had become a very remote and almost undefinable political entity.

A new phase of this long evolution is now emerging. I have described it as the twilight of civil servants. I do not mean by this expression that the Establishment is following the same pattern as the Cabinet and tends to become another symbol of power. What I do mean is that it will have to share the monopolistic influence it had in the past on ministers with others, namely the public, the intellectual community, the private member of Parliament, and the press. In other words, the reality of power will be less concentrated in one group; it will be more diffuse.

What will happen to ministers in this complex new world? Generally speaking, a dependent becomes more independent when he has several masters instead of one. But I am inclined to think that this will not be true in this case. Ministers will have to devote a growing portion of their time to their symbolic role. They will find it harder to reconcile their different loyalties. In the process of reaching a compromise which will make their masters at least equally dissatisfied, their true personality will be weakened and their convictions will become blurred. Their diverse activities will affect their health and their private lives. In the outward show which will be theirs as symbols of power, they will try to wear a mask to hide their tiredness and their boredom.

One might ask who will want to become a minister under such dismal conditions. My answer would be that we do not need to worry: to many people and to a great number of politicians, the symbols of power are more attractive than the reality of power.

# 18 Royal Commissions in the General Policy Process and in Federal-Provincial Relations*

## G. Bruce Doern

Royal commissions have been cynically called "Canada's biggest industry."[1] While everyone from politicians to farmers and from bankers to union leaders has alternately damned and praised particular commissions, there has been surprisingly little analysis made by Canadian political scientists about royal commissions even as a part of the *general* policy process, much less about their utility in federal-provincial relations.

This paper will attempt to draw some conclusions about their future role in the policy process, generally, and in federal-provincial relations in particular.

The royal commission "technique" of developing policy has essentially three qualities: it is public, *ad hoc,* and investigatory in its operation. By "public" is meant its usefulness in sweeping into the policy process outside or non-governmental, or non-civil service, participants. Implicit in the "public" quality is the desire to introduce a degree of independent and alternative sources of information and opinion about policy problems other than could be provided by inside governmental advisers. The royal commission is *"ad hoc"* in the sense that it is momentary or discontinuous

---

* G. Bruce Doern, "The Role of Royal Commissions in the General Policy Process and in Federal-Provincial Relations," *Canadian Public Administration*, Vol. 10, No. 4 (December, 1967), pp. 417-33 (reprinted and abridged by permission of author and publisher).
[1] *Financial Post* (Sept. 1, 1962), p. 3.

policy machinery which is dismantled once it has carried out its investigatory function on a specific policy topic, and has no responsibility
whatever to implement its own recommendations. It is because of the
absence of an "execution" function that the royal commission is distinguished by its "investigatory" quality. If the totality of the policy process
can be viewed as a three-stage spectrum involving a research or investigatory stage followed by a decision stage and then an implementation
stage, it will be readily seen that the royal commission plays only a
"pre-decision" or investigatory role.

If the above is a generally accurate portrayal of the essential qualities
of the royal commission technique, it stands in vivid contrast, at a purely
general level, to the essential qualities of the modern policy process and
more specifically of federal-provincial policy relations, which are characterized by dependence on "intragovernmental" (that is, nonpublic in the
sense intended earlier) participants and advisers, by a "continuous" rather
than *ad hoc* approach, and by involvement with the whole spectrum of
the policy process – its investigatory, decision-making and implementation
stages.

There are, of course, exceptions to the general description given above.
Generally, however, this paper seeks to establish the incompatibility of the
royal commission technique with most of the modern policy problems that
have to be faced, especially in the realm of federal-provincial relations.
More specifically, based on both the inherent qualities of the royal commission technique and recent developments in policy machinery, in line
with the analysis above, it finds a relatively limited utility to the royal
commission technique. The thesis it proposes is threefold. First, the need
to have continuous policy machinery will mean that more and more these
aspects of continuity will have to be satisfied within the civil service in the
form of more elaborate research staff and interdepartmental machinery.
Second, to retain and perhaps expand the democratic need for outside
participants in the policy process, that is, to preserve independent sources
of analysis and research, one of the best hopes is the development of permanently endowed research institutes centred at Canadian universities.
Third, royal commissions can be most effectively used in narrower non-
recurring areas of policy development, where problems are more in the
nature of special cases or specific disputes.

There have been a number of one-man royal commissions in Canada.
This is no doubt because of the prevalence and influence of the opinion,
until recent times, that all royal commissions are judicial inquests. Related
to this has been a heavy reliance on the Bench for chairmen and on the
Bar for commission counsel. The Bilingualism and Biculturalism Commission and other recent examples indicate that this highly formal judi-

cial type is giving way to a new type. There were inklings of this as early as the Rowell-Sirois Commission, but evolution of the new approach has significantly accelerated in the past eight years. The new composition and procedure has been characterized by turning for personnel elsewhere than to the Bench and Bar, and to the use of broadly based social science research staffs instead of the public hearing as the prime method of gathering evidence, thus reflecting the social nature of the subjects under study and the need for people educated in the social science disciplines.

The implications of the relative decline in importance of public hearings and the new reliance by the most important recent royal commissions on their own staffs as the major source of information are important. The assembling of teams of experts into a staff of several hundred for a two- or three-year period places the staff of a royal commission in a quasi-departmental status: "The government now recognizes this fact and Royal Commissions of this size are treated for purposes of the Financial Administration Act as a 'department'."[2]

With the commission under the more direct control of Treasury Board, there is raised the question of the traditional independence of commissions, which may now be jeopardized. The important feature here is that even if, on a *de facto* basis, independence seems assured, nevertheless a suspicion of the commission as being another department of the government may develop.

A further problem is the relationship between commissioners and their research teams. The use of public hearings as the sole means of collecting facts allowed the practice of appending the verbatim reports to the commission report. The reader could weave his way through and perhaps follow the thought processes of the commissioners in reaching their final conclusions. This tabling of the relevant pros and cons becomes harder when the data, already interpreted by a research staff, reach the commissioners' ears and eyes, second hand. "Much of the evidence has to be taken on faith and a correspondingly heavy reliance has to be placed on the objectivity and abilities of the researchers to ensure that all relevant information does get up to the commission."[3]

This problem is really a variation of the familiar theme of ministerial responsibility. The more royal commissions become like small departments of government, the more important the staff-commission relationship becomes. The question then arises whether they *should* become departments or permanent research agencies attached to a department.

2 J. E. Hodgetts, "Should Canada be De-Commissioned?" *Queen's Quarterly*, Vol. 70 (Winter, 1964), p. 484.
3 *Ibid.*, p. 485.

Professor Hodgetts suggests that "the more a commission takes on the characteristics of a conventional department, the more the temporary staff of investigators have to accept the status of civil servants."[4]

When recent commissions in areas of recurring social and economic problems show a pronounced reliance on closed staffs rather than open public hearings, it may be thought that the democratization of the policy process, especially in this technological age of cumulative change, might be better served by an open "hearing", a publishing right being given to dissenting views, or the development of alternative sources of policy "intelligence" by outside participants. There is a certain inevitability about the down-grading of public hearings and their ability to make a relevant contribution to policy formation in complex social and economic fields. Hodgetts thinks this is not an "anti-democratic" development, but I submit that it could well become "undemocratic", should royal commissions, as applied to the great recurring social and economic policies, become more and more like departments of government and thereby turn over to the civil service virtually the whole of the policy process. An important aspect of the democratic policy-making process is that it be shared between groups committed to the government and other uncommitted experts from outside. There ought to be ways by which the latter group can be continuously a part of the policy process so that their opinions may be known during the process of policy-making and not merely after the policy is set. In this connection the political parties, especially the opposition party, research institutes, and parliamentary resources have very special responsibilities.

But even where policy has been implemented, there emerges one characteristic of the royal commission technique which calls its effectiveness in question. One criticism levelled at the Glassco Commission and levelled at others as well is that, once the commission has made its recommendations, there is conferred on it no responsibility or machinery to carry out the proposals. T. H. McLeod was highly critical of the use of "outsiders" to research what only "insiders" can thoroughly do: "The Royal Commission approach to administrative reorganization creates an irreparable breach in the course of a process which to be fully effective must be continuous and single."[5] In other words, the commissioners who *are* convinced of the merits of the proposals they are making leave the scene, and it remains for some third party or coordinating agency to convince and convert the insiders in government to the proposals the out-

---

[4] *Ibid.*, p. 487.
[5] T. H. McLeod, "Glassco Commission Report," *Canadian Public Administration*, Vol. 6, No. 4 (December, 1963), p. 390.

siders have made. Why not, the argument goes, leave out this first and wasteful step and provide the government itself with the necessary research resources, especially on recurring social and economic problems? There can be little doubt of the general logic of this argument. Indeed, the Glassco Commission itself, with respect to the need for continuing research on administrative organization and techniques, recommended that such a permanent function be assigned to a special division of Treasury Board.[6]

The assumption of a department-like posture by these recent commissions, coupled with the rapidly expanding role of the Privy Council Planning Secretariat, seems to be sweeping the policy process, relatively speaking, more and more within the ambit of the government itself. This has a necessary and desirable aspect, provided that there develop alternative policy resources outside the governmental sphere.

Serious federal-provincial repercussions are apt to be felt not so much at the royal commission or investigatory stage, but rather at the implementation stage. In these more direct confrontations, it no longer matters who made the recommendations because the adjustment and implementation must take place directly within the policy machinery of federal-provincial relations. The simple recognition of this seems to be leading this process to its logical conclusion of bringing the totality of these complex recurring problems wholly within the ambit of intergovernmental machinery, in the hope of avoiding some of the delay and perhaps also some of the misunderstandings that arise when royal commissions carry out the first stage of the policy process and are left with no responsibility whatever for the decision and implementation stages.

## Conclusions

Although royal commissions have been used and have significantly affected federal-provincial relations, the effect has been of an indirect nature. The development of more permanent federal-provincial machinery and also general policy machinery, such as the new Transportation Commission, not to mention more elaborate interdepartmental and staff machinery in the federal and provincial governments, seems to be a recognition of the inherent defects or inadequacies of the commission technique. An *ad hoc* public, investigatory technique is not adequate to face a modern federal state's policy problems, most of which are of a continuous recurring nature and which involve the expanded participation of civil servants within the several governments.

---

6 *Royal Commission on Government Organization* (Ottawa, Queen's Printer), p. 64; see also address by the Hon. E. J. Benson, "What has been Happening to the Organization of the Government of Canada?" (January, 1967).

The fact that most policy problems are of this nature suggests two corollaries. First, there still remain many areas of policy that are non-recurring. In these situations, royal commissions can still serve useful functions. For royal commission functions other than the conduct of research there are likely to remain several areas of policy, especially in the socio-cultural field, where the politics and democracy of the policy process may make royal commissions desirable. For example, in my judgment, the recently appointed Commission on the Status of Women is appropriately a subject for royal commission study, precisely because it conforms to the nature of an *ad hoc* investigation.

A second corollary is that, if broad recurring areas of public policy are to be swept wholly within the ambit of governmental machinery, then there ought to be complementary and alternative sources of intelligence and there ought to be outside or public participants to reinforce or replace the desirable openness which the royal commission technique provided. If there is a need for greater non-governmental participation in the policy process, then it is the other policy techniques, like legislative and Senate committees, political parties, and research institutes, which we must call upon. Since each of these covers a wide range in itself, only some broad observations about them, so as to place the total policy process in perspective, is undertaken here.

It is by no means coincidental that the development of standing committees of the House of Commons has taken place in precisely the broad areas of recurring social and economic problems noted for royal commissions. Standing committees and special committees have been used frequently since Confederation as a means of conducting *ad hoc* inquiries. In recent years, the development of legislative committees to handle recurring problems has undergone marginal improvement, but continued reliance on royal commissions attests to the inadequacies of the legislative committee system as a suitable complement and/or substitute. The committees are generally too large, lack research resources, and take up a tremendous amount of time for members of Parliament. They are, furthermore, limited in life to the duration of the parliamentary session and are crammed into an already burdensome parliamentary agenda. The need to stay in Ottawa normally does not allow committee members to canvass public opinion through public hearings, which is a considerable disability in pluralistic Canada. It is doubtful that significant improvement in legislative committees as an alternative can be expected, save perhaps that of improving the research resources available to them so as to make them more like the more effective American congressional committee system. The likelihood of longer parliamentary sessions, however, coupled with the inevitable dominance of committees by Cabinet and the Government party, seems to impose permanent long-term disadvantages on the legislative committee system in Canada. Improvements can be made, but it appears doubtful that, relatively speaking, a strengthened committee system can lead to a more democratic balance in the policy process.

More promising for seeking out alternative policy making techniques might be Senate committees. In fact, recent improvements in the Senate committee technique, such as the provision of research assistants, have led to some matters, for example, the Senate Report on Aging, to be referred there rather than creating new royal commissions. The dominance of the governing party seems less pressing in Senate committees and even in joint Commons-Senate committees. The opportunities for a relatively nonpartisan long-range inquiry, unhurried by cramped agendas, constitute a real advantage.

As to the role of our political parties in the policy process, suffice it to say that the policy techniques of the political parties, especially of the opposition parties, could be considerably improved. The unavailability of financial resources to support continuous research, especially between election periods, is the great drawback. While it is clear that the parties can do more, it may well be that the cost of securing the necessary resources for research are prohibitive.

A relatively untried policy-making alternative, research institutes centred at our universities, is worth examining. The need is for a permanent body of expertise related to recurring social and economic problems. The endowment of universities with the millions of dollars spent recently on department-like royal commissions would involve outsiders in the policy process. The outsiders who thus would become a part of the policy process would be precisely the outsiders most needed: the university academics and professionals, who have for so long clung to the myth that their role is not to be a part of the policy process but only a faithful critic of policy itself. Research institutes could also do much to restore the notion of genuine independence. If the cost to political parties of assembling their own expertise is indeed prohibitive, perhaps they could rely with some confidence on the institutes. In addition, as Professor Hodgetts remarks, "the fitful characteristics of Royal Commission inquiries could then be replaced by steadily cumulative results that would not be side-tracked simply because, as now, the sponsoring body has disappeared."[7]

Most of the recurring social and economic topics, e.g. resources, education, health, transportation, in some real way affect eleven governments in Canada. There is, therefore, superimposed on the urgent need for

---

[7] Hodgetts, *op. cit.*, p. 490.

viable general public policy-making techniques all the problems of inter-governmental relations and jurisdictions. The need is on a continuing basis. Research institutes seem worthy objects of public and private investment. The Queen's Institute of Intergovernmental Relations may be cited here. Other needed research institutes that might be suggested are one on transportation and one on urban problems.

The contention remains that the main problem with royal commissions is that they do not provide for a continuity between recommendation and execution. Therefore, is the policy process best served by keeping the research resources on a continuing basis *within* the government? To this end the civil service would be worthy of special attention. To those who despair about the capacity of our political parties and parliamentary committees to improve their role in the policy process, the great hope for a fluid method of policy techniques rests with the civil service and the new Co-ordinating and Planning Secretariat of the Privy Council. The development of a vigorous cross-communication and dialogue between and among departments will doubtless be a valuable complement to the policy process. But this kind of private dialogue arouses suspicion or at least skepticism. If the royal commission technique in the area of recurring social and especially economic problems is to be swept away and replaced by permanent research and coordinating agencies within both levels of government, it is essential that such a process be accompanied by a comparable development in our nongovernmental research and policy-making resources, especially by the political parties and by the creation of well endowed research institutes.

Lest these concluding remarks leave the impression that the royal commission should be a thing of the past, let it be clearly reiterated that the royal commission is of unquestioned value in many areas of policy-making and investigation. It is still quite crucial in its educational and safety-valve function. But recent developments in composition and procedures should make us look into alternative and complementary methods of policy development, both in the general policy process and with respect to federal-provincial relations in particular.

# Part Three

*READINGS*

Bieler, J. H., "The Role of the Deputy Minister: I." *Canadian Public Administration*, Vol. 4, No. 4 (December, 1961), pp. 352-56.

Bridges, The Right Hon. Lord, "Relations entre les Ministres et les Chefs permanents des ministères." *Canadian Public Administration*, Vol. 7, No. 3 (September, 1964), pp. 282-94.

Bridges, The Right Hon. Lord, "The Relationships between Ministers and the Permanent Departmental Head." *Canadian Public Administration*, Vol. 7, No. 3 (September, 1964), pp. 269-81.

Burns, R. M., "The Role of the Deputy Minister: II." *Canadian Public Administration*, Vol. 4, No. 4 (December, 1961), pp. 357-62.

"Déclaration de principes sur les droits civils dans le fonctionnarisme." *Relations Industrielles*, Vol. 14 (October, 1959), pp. 598-603.

Corbett, D. C., "The Pressure Group and the Public Interest." *Proceedings of the Fifth Annual Conference*, Toronto, Institute of Public Administration of Canada, 1953, pp. 185-95.

Dawson, Helen Jones, "Consumer Association of Canada." *Canadian Public Administration*, Vol. 6, No. 1 (March, 1963), pp. 92-118.

Dawson, Helen Jones, "Interest Group: The Canadian Federation of Agriculture." *Canadian Public Administration*, Vol. 3, No. 2 (June, 1960), pp. 134-49.

Dawson, Helen Jones, "Relations between Farm Organizations and the Civil Service in Canada and Great Britain." *Canadian Public Administration*, Vol. 10, No. 4 (December, 1967), pp. 450-70.

Deutsch, J. J., "Parliament and the Civil Service." *Queen's Quarterly*, Vol. 63 (Winter, 1957), pp. 565-73.

Deutsch, J. J., "Some Thoughts on the Public Service." *Canadian Journal of Economics and Political Science*, Vol. 23, No. 1 (February, 1957), pp. 83-89.

Doern, G. Bruce, "The Role of the Royal Commission in the General Policy Process and in Federal-Provincial Relations." *Canadian Public Administration*, Vol. 10, No. 4 (December, 1967), pp. 417-33.

Dussault, René, "Relationship between the Nature of the Acts of the Administration and Judicial Review: Quebec and Canada." *Canadian Public Administration*, Vol. 10, No. 3 (September, 1967), pp. 298-322.

Hicks, H. D., "Civil Servants and Politicians: a Defence of Politicians." *Canadian Public Administration*, Vol. 6, No. 3 (September, 1963), pp. 261-73.

Hodgetts, J. E., "Liberal and Bureaucrat." *Queen's Quarterly*, Vol. 62 (Summer, 1955), pp. 176-83.

Hodgetts, J. E., "Public Power and Ivory Power," in Trevor Lloyd and Jack McLeod, *Agenda 1970: Proposals for a Creative Politics* (Toronto, University of Toronto Press, 1968), pp. 256-80.

Hodgetts, J. E., "The Civil Service and Policy Formation." *Canadian Journal of Economics and Political Science*, Vol. 23, No. 4 (November, 1957), pp. 467-79.

Hughes, S. H. S., "The Public Official—Parliament, Public and the Press." *Canadian Public Administration*, Vol. 3, No. 4 (December, 1960), pp. 289-98.

Jewett, Pauline, "The Political and Administrative Aspects of Policy Formation," in T. Brewis et al., *Canadian Economic Policy*, 2nd ed. (Toronto, The Macmillan Company of Canada, 1965), pp. 350-57.

Johnson, A. W., "The Role of the Deputy Minister: III." *Canadian Public Administration*, Vol. 4, No. 4 (December, 1961), pp. 363-73.

Kernaghan, W. D. K., "The Political Rights and Activities of Canadian Public

Servants," in A. M. Willms and W. D. K. Kernaghan, eds., *Public Administration in Canada* (Toronto, Methuen Publications, 1968), pp. 446-54.

MacFarlane, R. O., "Freedoms and Limitations of the Public Servant." *Canadian Education*, Vol. 11 (September, 1956), pp. 65-71.

McKeough, W. Darcy, "The Relations of Ministers and Civil Servants." *Canadian Public Administration*, Vol. 12, No. 1 (Spring, 1969), pp. 1-8.

Mallory, J. R., "The Minister's Office Staff: an Unreformed Part of the Public Service." *Canadian Public Administration*, Vol. 10, No. 1 (March, 1967), pp. 25-34.

Shoyama, T. K., "Advisory Committees in Administration." *Proceedings of the Ninth Annual Conference*, Toronto, Institute of Public Administration of Canada, 1957, pp. 145-53.

Taylor, K. W., "Pressure Groups in Administration." *Proceedings of the Fifth Annual Conference*, Toronto, Institute of Public Administration of Canada, 1953, pp. 155-206.

Taylor, M. G., "Role of the Medical Profession in the Formulation and Execution of Public Policy." *Canadian Journal of Economics and Political Science*, Vol. 26, No. 1 (February, 1960), pp. 108-27.

Thorburn, H. G., "Pressure Groups in Canadian Politics: Recent Revisions of the Anti-Combines Legislation." *Canadian Journal of Economics and Political Science*, Vol. 30, No. 2 (May, 1964), pp. 157-74.

# PART FOUR

# Administrative Responsibility

The meanings assigned to the elusive concept of administrative responsibility include, among others, efficiency, consistency, responsiveness, competence, and accountability. Any attempt to capture the essence of the concept in a brief statement is therefore an impracticable task. A more fruitful endeavor is to explore the means of achieving administrative responsibility through the adoption of instruments to control the exercise of discretionary authority by public servants. All selections in this part set out specific proposals for the use of such control devices.

Eric Hehner begins by describing the scope and the danger of the continued expansion of delegated legislative and judicial powers to the bureaucracy. Peter Silcox is concerned with the increase in bureaucratic authority resulting from the proliferation of boards and commissions enjoying varying degrees of independence from political control. Donald C. Rowat examines the institution of the Ombudsman as an instrument of control and assesses its existing and potential adaptation to Canadian governments.

J. A. Corry's statement on the future of public law provides an effective conclusion to this part and to the book. He sees clearly the threat to individual and collective rights from the irreversible expansion of discretionary administrative powers. He contends that application of the rule of law to the contemporary administrative process can achieve the necessary reconciliation of public power and private right.

# 19 Growth of Discretions— Decline of Accountability*

## Eric Hehner

The functions of the public service have changed in a fundamental way which requires re-appraisal of the positions of Parliament and of the courts of law. This change has happened so quietly that its extent, its basic nature, and its significance to our system of government have not yet been widely recognized. The administrator has gained vastly wider powers and the legislature is losing both knowledge of, and effective control over, the way in which the powers it has conferred are exercised. This has created a new relationship between the individual and the state, and is contributing to the sterilization of Parliament.

Parliament, the public service, and the courts of law were designed for limited functions of government. The ideal of legislation was to be definitive and precise, and to leave little to the imagination or to opinion. Our forefathers undoubtedly fell far short of this ideal, but the ideal was there. The public service performed administrative and service functions. The courts were adjudicators of facts and defenders of injured individuals from other individuals or from the state. Judicial decisions were made under a rule of law with the rules fixed beforehand and equally applicable to all.

Government today is expected to offer direction and to execute policies

---

* Eric Hehner, "Growth of Discretions – Decline of Accountability" (reprinted and abridged with permission of author from an unpublished address delivered to the Ottawa Regional Group of the Institute of Public Administration of Canada on November 24, 1965).

of a positive nature – to be an active participant in economic and social affairs, not just a writer of rules and an umpire. Had our economic and social structures and the technology on which they in part rest been relatively static, a rule of law as known in the past might have provided an adequate mechanism to enable government to play an increased role. However, the expansion of the scale of economic processes has been great enough to produce differences of nature, not just of size. It has made necessary the use of discretions by governmental authority, which cannot be exercised by Parliament itself.

The activities of government have changed to meet the needs of the times, but our political and legal structure has failed to keep pace. There has been increasing delegation of authority by Parliament to the cabinet, to departments and boards, and to nameless public servants. Since the government is playing a more active and positive role at a time of rapidly changing technology, changing patterns of domestic and international trade, and changing social viewpoints, it cannot spell out in statutes all of the provisions and exemptions needed to look after the innumerable variations of modern requirements. Our need for greater flexibility in administration has been growing, and the location of responsibility for executive, legislative, and judicial functions has become somewhat vague. The activities of departments of government are no longer separable into neat, mutually-exclusive areas of interest. As the functions and direct participation of government have extended, the machinery of administration has become more complicated and has ceased to be merely administrative.

We have changed the activities of government to an extent that makes even more discretionary powers inevitable. We have provided for many such powers, and at an accelerating pace. However, instead of entering wholeheartedly into the creation of discretions with our eyes open to its implications and needs and simultaneously providing machinery to prevent the abuse of discretionary powers, we have tried to pretend that there has been no basic change. We have left discretions to be exercised as much in the shadows of secrecy as possible. It is getting more difficult to tell where lawmaking stops and administration starts. It is getting harder to place responsibility for actions (or lack of them) among the multiplicity of government agencies now involved. Even greater use of discretionary powers may be essential but these powers carry with them potential for abuse unless there are surrounding safeguards.

It is now the norm for a statute to delegate authority to make regulations to achieve objectives which have been expressed in very general terms. If regulations extend only to details of mechanical procedures, no real discretionary powers are delegated. However, where the statutory provisions are only a skeleton and it is left to regulations to say "what, where, when, why, how and who," then we have created meaningful discretionary powers and should examine the mechanisms available to review the exercise of these powers. When regulations are issued by the Governor-in-Council, or even by a minister of the Crown, there is at least a degree of accountability for this first step. Where the power is conferred upon a board or commission, review of its exercise becomes more difficult and remote. However, if the discretions have been consciously delegated to a named body directly responsible to the legislature, there is at least a placing of responsibility. If persons or bodies possessed of delegated powers re-delegate them, we come to a state that a Deputy Minister recently described as "dispersed discretions". When discretionary judgments are not the result of a conscious act which has placed the responsibility upon a named person or body, but are the result of pretending that matters of opinion are matters of fact, we are further into an area of trouble.

The courts have been the traditional safeguard for the rights of one individual against another or against the state, but the courts were designed to adjudicate matters which at least purport to be issues of fact in relation to pre-established law. Courts lack both the powers and in most cases the capacity to substitute their judgment for opinions which others have been empowered to express. In essence, the traditional courts are incapable of playing a constructive part in the newly developing functions of government, where exercise of discretions is required. For this reason positive action has frequently been taken by legislatures to exclude the exercise of delegated discretions from the jurisdiction of the courts, if it was found or suspected that the courts might be in a position to intervene.

J. A. Corry, disturbed by the multiplication of administrative discretions, has asserted that

> "As far as machinery goes, the most hopeful possibility is the establishment of special standing committees of the House of Commons with the express function of watching over the area of administration covered by particular departments of government, committees which would be entitled to take up complaints of aggrieved persons and to secure facts and explanations about the course of administration from civil servants. .... In the mammoth government departments of today, there is constant danger that the minister will become the prisoner of his officials. Because the exercise of discretionary powers must be controlled by Parliament if they are to be controlled at all, it is necessary to get the House of Com-

mons closer to the complexities of administration. This is not a new idea, but its importance for the control of discretionary powers is immense".[1]

It is significant that of nineteen bills passed by the House of Commons during the third Session of the twenty-sixth Parliament ten acts did not confer discretions and nine acts did. Of the ten which conferred no discretions, three were passing supplementary estimates, one provided for retirement of members of the Senate, one authorized construction of a nine-mile railway extension, one amended the Army Benevolent Fund Act, and four were routine amendments of other statutes which merely extended time limits and did not add new discretions to those already conferred in the Acts being amended.

Among those bills conferring discretionary authority were Bills C 104 and C 129. Bill C 104 gave a Minister, on terms and conditions to be approved by the Governor-in-Council, the power to increase by almost one billion dollars the funds available to Central Mortgage and Housing Corporation. Parliament did not say that this rather large amount of money should or should not be made available, or the terms and conditions of its availability. Parliament merely abdicated its right to control this amount and left it up to Cabinet and the Minister to do as they pleased.

Bill C 129, the Area Development Incentives Act, is replete with phrases which leave the real operating provisions to be defined by persons other than the legislators who passed the statute. In this case, there is not one page of the seven pages of the Act which does not confer discretions. The capital costs in respect of which a development grant may be authorized are to be "determined by the Minister". The approved areas are to be "designated after the commencement of this Act". There are loose phrases like "necessary components", "substantial progress", "all reasonable speed", "may be necessarily incidental", "reasonably and responsibly," and others equally indefinable. There is repeated use of "the Minister may prescribe", "the Minister may allow", "if the Minister is of the opinion", "when the Minister is satisfied". There is nothing in this Act that is not discretionary.

In addition to legislative acts of this nature, there is the whole area of "Rules, orders, regulations, by-laws or proclamations which are made by regulation-making authorities in the exercise of a legislative power" – commonly known as Statutory Orders and Regulations. In any year these are numbered in the thousands, and not only delegate authority but frequently re-delegate it. For example, revised Veterans' Land Act Regu-

---

[1] J. A. Corry, "The Prospects for the Rule of Law," *Canadian Journal of Economics and Political Science*, Vol. 21, No. 4 (November, 1955), p. 412.

lations, published in the *Canada Gazette* of June 9, 1965 contain such judgment phrases as "typical Canadian standard of living," and others similarly indefinable. Authority to exercise judgments and make determinations is delegated not only to "The Director, the Veterans' Land Act" but to "District Superintendents" and to "any person authorized to act on behalf of" such superintendents. The judgments these officers are called upon to make are value judgments; the repetitive references to "in the opinion of" and use of the permissive word "may" leave the public servants in the position of autocrats whether or not they desire such powers.

As a second example of many which could be given, Revised Old Age Security Regulations published in the July 14 issue of the *Gazette* specifically state that certain discretions shall vest in a Director. The Director may in turn "delegate to Regional Directors any duty, power or discretion conferred on him by these regulations". The Director is then given almost absolute powers over the essentials of qualifying for assistance. He is not bound to accept any evidence respecting such a factual matter as age. He may, but does not have to, submit a disputed case to an appeal tribunal. The applicant is not provided with a right of appeal. The Director is made the judge of what is in the best interest of the pensioner.

The statutes used as examples have the merit of being published documents. In addition, there is a large area of unpublished Orders-in-Council and Ministerial prescriptions. There is also the broad field of so-called administrative decisions (or lack of decisions) which are equally exercises of discretion. These are by nature difficult to deal with in public, because they frequently involve decisions relating to private and confidential affairs of individual persons or companies. One can only learn of the details through a confidential relationship to those affected. However, these unpublished Orders-in-Council, Ministerial Prescriptions, or administrative decisions are frequently of general application and remain unknown to many persons affected by them because they are not published.

The magnitude of the developments described has been generally unrecognized. Most people still think that Parliament makes the laws except for small details; that public servants just administer; and that those exercising delegated discretions are accountable for their actions in fact as well as in theory to the elected representatives of the people. The rule of law as we knew it until World War II has just about gone and effective accountability to Parliament has been lost over a wide area of governmental activity.

Perhaps what has happened has been inevitable; it may even be desirable – but not as long as we pretend that nothing has really happened to change the old order. If we permit the proliferation of powers – dispersed discretions – without setting up an effective mechanism to supervise the exercise of these powers, a free community will not long survive.

Unless we find some way of bringing Parliament back into the picture, its individual members, legislating only in generalities and without effective means of seeing how their servants are acting, are reduced to comparative impotence. The Parliamentary Special Committee on Procedure and Organization which reported in December 1964 recognized the joint problems of growth of discretions being exercised by appointed officials and loss of effective control by Parliament. It attempted to deal with the situation by recommending that there be established a Standing Committee on Delegated Legislation. The purpose of this proposed Standing Committee was described as follows:

> "The function of this committee would be to act as a "watchdog" over the executive in its use of the powers conferred by statute, with the duty of reporting to Parliament any tendency on the part of the executive to exceed its authority. The committee's terms of reference should exclude it from considering the merits of or the policy behind delegated legislation, but it would be expected to draw the attention of Parliament to any regulations or instruments which impose a charge on public revenues, which confer immunity from challenge in the courts, which have an unauthorized retroactive effect, which reveal an unusual or unexpected use of a statutory power, or which otherwise exceed the authority delegated by the parent statute."[2]

This recommendation was not accepted by the Government.[3]

Delegated legislation is sufficiently significant that it deserves a special mechanism for review of its exercise. Unless members of Parliament fulfil this function, Parliament as we have known it will become relatively impotent. Some public servants have questioned whether members of Parliament can be expected to approach review of the exercise of dis-

---

[2] *Journals* (Commons) (December 14, 1964), p. 988.

[3] [Editor's Note] On September 30, 1968, the Government appointed a Special Committee on Statutory Instruments "to consider and, from time to time report on procedures for the review by this house of instruments made in virtue of any statute of the parliament of Canada". *Debates* (Commons) (September 30, 1968), p. 577. When introducing the motion to the House on September 24, D. S. Macdonald pointed to the Committee's restricted terms of reference. The legislation does not "set up a standing committee on delegated legislation itself". The Committee is to examine Canadian practice in the area of "statutory instruments or delegated legislation to ascertain whether it would be advisable to set up some kind of procedure so that this house, more particularly through a committee, could make a better scrutiny of these subsidiary instruments. . . ." The Committee is not to deal with such other means of controlling administrative action as "providing legal rights of recourse, either by appeal to the regular court system or by means of prerogative writs," or "the Scandinavian system of the ombudsman". *Debates* (Commons) (September 24, 1968), pp. 438-39.

cretions in a non-partisan manner. They seem to feel that politicians will refuse to distinguish between the essentially political acts of determining policy and voting for legislative programmes, and the essentially non-partisan function of studying how powers delegated by legislation are being exercised. Perhaps the question might be phrased – can members forget party politics long enough to be objective in protecting the rights of the individual to the end that there is equal justice for all, and efficient, non-discriminatory application of the law? This is a function which the courts cannot fulfil in relation to the exercise of delegated discretions. If members of Parliament cannot, or will not, do this job through committees established for this purpose, then we should at least abandon the pretence that they are able to do so now.

# 20 The Proliferation of Boards and Commissions*

## Peter Silcox

The expansion of government activities has had three important results. First, the contacts between governments, government and non-governmental organizations, and government and the general population have all been made much more complex. Second, far more professionals and specialists have been brought into government and, because many of their activities are difficult for the layman to understand, the problem of political control has become more complicated. Third, new administrative forms, whose relationship to the normal departmental structure is difficult to work out, have proliferated.

Many of these changes have been brought about by political parties explicitly committed to the proposition that big government poses a threat to the best interests of society. This general view has also been shared by a large majority of the population, at least in North America. Despite these general outlooks popularly elected governments have gone on expanding their activities and there can be no doubt that they have done so, as they themselves claim, under pressure from public opinion. Practically every group in society demands government protection or assistance in its "special" case *despite* the fact its members share the general feeling of disquiet about the expanding role of government. This

* Peter Silcox, "The Proliferation of Boards and Commissions" in Trevor Lloyd and Jack McLeod, *Agenda 1970: Proposals for a Creative Politics* (Toronto, University of Toronto Press, 1968), pp. 115-34 (reprinted and abridged by permission of author and publisher).

ambivalence has had an important effect on politicians when they have considered the best administrative structure for dealing with new governmental responsibilities. The semi-independent public agency has a number of attractive features for them. It can give the appearance of being a politically independent corporate body allowed to operate in the manner of the allegedly efficient profit-maximizing private corporation. This structure also has the advantage of making it easier to give interested groups a partnership role in the government's work. In general there can be little doubt that, whatever the realities behind the form, the use of this type of agency does appear to the public to depoliticize the government's role and also to some extent conceal the overall expansion of its power and influence.

Three types of government intervention and agency can be distinguished. First, departments directly under the day-to-day control and supervision of a member of the government. Second, semi-independent public agencies created and given policy goals by the government, which retain some control of the general size and shape of their administrative structure. Third, government-assisted bodies dependent, often to a considerable degree, on government assistance and financial help but not created by an official government initiative; these have a much larger degree of control over their long-term aims and have considerable independence of outside control in organizing their internal organization and procedures.

There are a very large number of semi-independent agencies in existence at both the federal and provincial levels in Canada. Most of them have been established in the past twenty-five years. Among the approximately fifty agencies at the federal level, the most notable group is that of Crown corporations. A number of these, like Air Canada and the CNR, are as large or larger than the most important departments, and others, like the War Veterans Allowance Board, are of more limited significance. In Ontario, there were about fifty "ministerial agencies" in 1968. Some examples of Ontario semi-independent agencies are Ontario Hydro, the Hospital Services Commission, and the much smaller Ontario Highway Transport Board and the Ontario Racing Commission.

The founders of semi-independent agencies have given all kinds of reasons for setting them up. They range in sophistication from C. D. Howe's explanation that a commission should take the form of a corporation because that's the way they are operated around Ottawa to the administrative-technical accounts found in textbooks on public administration. These books explain that the semi-independent form is most useful when, first, the type of administrative flexibility associated with private corporations demands the avoidance of many of the administrative control

procedures used in the departmental structure; second, the direct interference of politicians with the day-to-day operations is to be minimized;
third, the co-operation of specialists who are often unfavourably disposed
to the idea of becoming civil servants is required; fourth, swift action is
needed in areas in which the departments have no previous experience.

To bring some order into the chaos of the new areas of government
activity, students and administrators have classified agencies according to
administrative-technical criteria. Two standard criteria have been used:
(1) type of activity, which has led to the establishment of sub-classes
such as proprietary, administrative, judicial, quasi-judicial, and so on;
(2) the extent of direct government control as attested to by formal
provisions establishing the agency; its freedom in raising funds and the
security of tenure of its directors for example. This type of classification
can be seen in the Canada Financial Administration Act of 1951.[1]

These classifications appear neat and definitive and they have a kind
of non-political air about them acceptable to many public administrators.
They are also almost useless if one is concerned with the question of how
political power is exercised and the determination of the nature and
extent of political responsibility. However, there is evidence to show these
arguments often are in the minds of politicians establishing semi-independent agencies, but they are not as decisive as public statements would
have us believe. The sceptical political scientist who investigates this area
soon discovers that a far wider range of considerations, mostly of a personal and political nature, come to the fore. He is forced to remember
that politicians have been at work. The political scientist discovers that
within the departmental framework he can find branches and divisions
which carry on activities of a commercial nature and that numerous ordinary civil servants are daily exercising judicial or quasi-judicial functions
which seem no different from those assigned to semi-independent agencies.
Then too, he discovers that all the formal protections for the independence of these agencies do not in practice protect them from the interference of politicians if a determined minister believes that the political
credit of the government he serves is at stake. Formal prescriptions are a
poor guide in attempting to determine who is responsible for the politically
significant decisions taken in the area of concern of a semi-independent
agency.

All these considerations lead to the suggestion of a different or additional set of reasons why the semi-independent form is sometimes attractive to politicians and a very different system of classification follows
from it. The overall expansion of government activities has brought

[1] See A. M. Willms, "Crown Agencies", p. 23.

governments more regularly into contact with each other, with privately operated public service organizations, and with powerful pressure groups. Their partnership in particular areas has often been consummated in semi-independent public bodies. Partnership may be desirable for a number of reasons. It may lead to greater efficiency, allow a government to limit its financial commitment or general political responsibility, or it may be the necessary price for active co-operation and political neutrality.

The creation of a semi-independent agency provides the opportunity for a government to minimize its financial support for a particular service from general taxation. Often such agencies are given the responsibility of being as financially self-sustaining as possible. Thus the collection of fees, charges, or contributions can be used to free the government from the financial burden. Contributions collected on a monthly basis by the Ontario Hospital Services Commission are quite clearly a simple poll tax, but they can be disguised as a form of insurance payment to an agency similar in appearance to a private insurance company. People in general are much less hostile to this kind of payment than to a simple poll tax or other regressive tax.

At a more immediately personal level a semi-independent agency might be established to remove from the area of responsibility of a particular minister a new service which the cabinet feels he is ill fitted to handle. One might also be established as a separate empire for a particularly powerful government supporter with a desire to press ahead in a given area. The desire to impress a special geographic area with the government's interest in it can sometimes be served by the creation of a development agency directed by local notables. Establishing agencies free from restrictions on hiring and firing partially makes up for the reduction of patronage caused by the merit system.

The most relevant classification of agencies will relate to the location of the effective political power to dictate the policies of the agency, to alter its form, or to prescribe its internal procedures. This criterion suggests that semi-independent agencies may be of three types. (1) Subordinate agencies: in relation to which one government has the effective power to set the policies, appoint and replace the directing board or commission, dictate the internal procedures, and change the legislation governing the agency's organization and powers. (2) Government partnership agencies: in this case none of the above changes can be made without changing the essential nature of the agency, unless the approval of governmental partners has been given, even if one level of government has statutory power over the agency. (3) Government group partnership agencies: where the government is inhibited in exercising any binding formal powers over the agency by the political requirement of satisfying the powerful groups that any proposed changes are not inimical to their interests. It might then be useful to classify agencies in each group according to "type of activity" or other more formal criteria.

This classification, like any other, is not a neat and tidy one. Some agencies may be difficult to fit into it with any certainty, and the same agency might be in different classes at different times. Its advantages are that it does take into account the question of where effective power to command the agency lies, and therefore where effective responsibility for its exercise should be fixed, and that it is not dependent on the purely formal criteria which are such a poor guide to the actual relationships between administrative bodies.

The conventional theory of the means for protecting the public interest assigns important roles to the government, the elected representatives of the people, and the group of individuals directing the agencies. The minister concerned has a number of tasks. It is his responsibility to lay down publicly the general role the government envisages for the agency and thus the general line of policy it must follow. He usually appoints board or commission members, and has final power of approval over investments, decisions, regulations, and procedural rules. With these responsibilities, and the knowledge gleaned from exercising them, the minister can ensure that the agency's work is co-ordinated with that of his own and other government departments. He can also answer in public, and in the legislature in particular, for the agency in those fields where he has responsibility. The task of the board is to use its specialist knowledge to run the day-to-day activities in an efficient manner, and to make decisions within the general policies laid down by the minister with the public interest in mind and without reference to any political considerations. The guarantee that they will concern themselves with the public interest lies in the appointment of honest, intelligent men, whose independent position safeguards them from immediate political pressures. The role of the legislature is to oversee the government's exercise of its responsibilities by using numerous opportunities open to it under the procedures of the legislature. Members can question the minister concerned, debate the regular reports made by the agency which are tabled in the assembly, and scrutinize and debate all legislation concerning the agency brought before the house. The legislature might also keep a more detailed check on these matters through the work of legislative committees. The legislature's responsibility is, of course, to ensure that all activities of the agency are in conformity with the public interest, but its specific control is confined to the area for which the minister is directly responsible.

This is all very comforting to the average citizen. With all these varied

groups hard at work to serve the public interest, the problems of co-
ordination, public responsibility, and protection of the individual citizen's
interests, all seem certain to be solved. But unfortunately it is not necessarily so. Immediately we begin to investigate the actual system, we find
serious discrepancies between the theory and the practice.

How do we define general overall policies? Do ministers always declare
them? What assurances have we that the minister is satisfied with limiting his interference in the operation of the agency to those powers given
to him under the legislation? Can we be assured that any powers of
financial supervision, for example, will not be used to determine the scale
and direction of day-to-day activities? In the case of agencies where more
than one governmental level is involved, how do we know that the responsible representatives will agree on the general lines of development the
agency should take? Is the minister knowledgeable enough and well disposed enough to other departments to ensure active efficient co-ordination
of government policies? Where agencies involving co-operation with
groups are concerned, is the minister more likely to be interested in
pacifying important political interests than serving the public good? None
of these questions can be answered in the affirmative with any confidence.
But have no fear. Remember, the minister is dealing with politically disinterested boards and commissions, and the legislature has an alert eye
on him.

Let us look at the boards and commissions and the legislature, then,
for confirmation of this. First, the boards. The first thing we notice here
is that there are a number of different categories of members, and one
cannot always be confident of their independence. Some members are
civil servants whose position or career prospects are directly dependent on
the minister. Some are members of the legislature, although none seem
to be members of political parties which oppose the government. Some
have long records of political service to political parties or, to be more
precise, to the party in power. Some are representatives of other governments or of non-government organizations. A minority are independent-
minded experts with no political record. They are a very mixed bunch,
and no board or commission is made up exclusively of one type of member. The one thing they have in common is that all were appointed
originally by politicians and ultimately all of them can be removed by
the same people who control the legislature, whatever kind of tenure they
might have.

Studies of the performance of legislative assemblies in the exercise of
the responsibilities assigned to them under the conventional theory have
reached conclusions that members are not well informed about the work
of semi-independent agencies. There is a paucity of information, the

members are very busy and have no adequate assistance in researching areas outside their most immediate political concerns, or they are complacent purveyors of the conventional theory.

The proliferation of semi-independent public agencies has led to three major problems which must be solved if the public interest is to be protected. First, the maintenance of efficiency requires that their activities be co-ordinated with those of other government bodies. Second, the protection of the right of citizens to have a say in how the government uses its powers requires that there be adequate opportunities for meaningful and informed discussion of their work. Third, the relations between the individual citizen and the agency must be conducted in such a way as to ensure that the former is aware of the reasons for decisions which affect him and is satisfied with the fairness of the procedures which have been followed. All of these problems occur in all public bureaucracies, but they are more acute in this sphere because physical and organizational separation from the departmental structure prevents the normal operation of the methods designed to overcome them.

The prime cause of these extra difficulties is the lack of readily available information on the exact relation of these agencies to the political executive and on their policies and practices. For example, it is impossible to judge if an individual citizen is being unfairly treated unless the aims, general policies, and procedures of an agency have been fully discussed and understood by a significant section of the public. Its conduct in individual cases can only be assessed against this general background. The failure to grasp this simple point has led to far too many cases in which there has been ill-informed criticism of particular agencies.

What changes then are necessary to ensure that the public interest is more adequately protected? The answer must, of course, vary with the type of agency; however, one major innovation is necessary which affects all of them. Far more studies of individual boards and commissions must be made and published. This means that academic investigators must be encouraged to take an interest in the field and their work must be facilitated by giving them free access to relevant material. If this is done, the complacency engendered by the conventional theory of control will quickly be dispelled. Disclosure alone will not deal with the problems I have outlined, but it is the necessary starting point in the search for solution.

Subordinate agencies are the first group we have to discuss. They range from departmental corporations, acknowledged in most cases to be part of the departmental structure, to quasi-judicial bodies with a reputation for their independence from political control. The one feature that these diverse agencies have in common is effective subordination to a minister, which means that a minister can get his own way over the policy the agency follows or the manner in which it is implemented without coming into direct conflict with powerful interest groups that have an institutionalized role in its work or with another level of government. The minister may in fact choose to give the subordinate agency a good deal of independence but he knows that he has the power to dominate, and so do those who direct the particular agency. Often this situation allows a minister to exercise power informally while stressing in public the formal limitations on his responsibility.

In this situation it is clearly the responsibility of the legislature to see that the government acts in the public interest. The link between power and responsibility is as clear as it is in the case of government departments. Modern legislatures are ill fitted at present to undertake the work of checking the work of departments, let alone the extra work involved in doing the same for subordinate agencies. The essential changes are not procedural: they are a willingness on the part of governments to make a clear statement of their policies and to lift the cloak of administrative secrecy, together with the provision of vastly improved facilities to the opposition for the collection of information and its expert assessment.

The most important single reform is the creation of a system of small specialist committees of members sitting not for just one session but throughout a parliament, with an expert staff partially under the control of opposition members. A committee without expert staff for the minority party is like a bird without wings. It has no hope of checking on the work of departments bulging with specialists under the command of the minister. For the same kind of reasons a committee on commissions, with or without a staff, is bound to be of very limited value. How can such a committee carry out a useful investigation of dozens of unrelated semi-independent agencies, let alone check how successfully they have co-ordinated their work with related agencies? The work of any board or commission must be investigated at the same time as that of related departments.

In the case of government partnership and government-group partnership agencies the effective political power, and therefore political responsibility, of a single minister is less easily fixed. The independence of these bodies is real because it is based not on formal considerations but on effective political power. In this situation special procedures may be developed which will more effectively result in the protection of the public interest. Two methods commend themselves to this writer: the "watchdog" continuous consultative committee and the committee of investigation. In both cases the "watchdogs" must have teeth. They must be chosen in part by people other than the concerned minister and they must have a specialist staff.

The consultative committee should have a continuous existence; it should have a small, partly expert membership, the assistance of staff, the power to summon papers and persons, and the right to publish reports at will. It might facilitate its work if a central office of consultative committees was established. With these facilities it could provide, as legislative committees should in their areas of responsibility, a continous commentary on the work of the agency and a centre where a citizen could take his complaints for discussion and if necessary for investigation. There might be some utility in attaching the office to that of the ombudsman, where that office exists. This would make the office's role more easily understood by the public and might lead to administrative efficiency by bringing together the staffs of offices with a similar role in the political system. It must be stressed, however, that the consultative committee should be concerned with general review as well as individual complaints.

An alternative or supplement to the consultative committee may be a periodic investigation by a small expert committee. Such an investigation if done on a regular schedule would have the advantage of being able to make a long-term assessment of the agency's work and of its success in co-ordination and dealing with the general public. In addition it might have some utility in checking the tendency of all administrative bodies to linger on in their old form long after it has ceased to be the most suitable one for the job.

Semi-independent agencies are public bodies, spending public money and using coercive powers in the name of the protection of the public interest. This circumstance gives the public the right to know precisely how they are spending the money and using the power. Then too, isn't the essence of responsible government the right of every citizen to have the information necessary to judge how the government is exercising its responsibilities? The special control procedures suggested here might serve to dissuade politicians from using the semi-independent form. If this did happen it would have the desirable effect of reducing the complexity of the public bureaucracy.

The legislature, equipped for its task in the way we have recommended, together with the other committees, would publicize the work of semi-independent agencies and provide the information on which the public could judge the extent to which they are serving the public interest, however that might be conceived by different people. The individual citizen would know where to go to get advice from informed people and whom to complain to if he was dissatisfied by his treatment at the hands of an agency. There would also be a considerable impetus to co-ordination if there was a real chance that political capital might be made out of a government's failings on that score.

# 21 The Ombudsman*

## Donald C. Rowat

Why has the Ombudsman idea spread so rapidly in recent years? A short answer is that the growth of the welfare state has made necessary new protections against bureaucratic mistakes and abuses of power. The Ombudsman is a novel and uniquely appropriate institution for dealing with the average citizen's complaints about unfair administrative action. It differs from our traditional methods of dealing with grievances and has important advantages over these methods.

Though the Ombudsman plan is new in the sense that it helps to meet the problem of an expanded bureaucracy in the modern welfare state, it is actually an old institution in Sweden where the Justitieombudsman (JO) was first appointed as an officer of the legislature under the Constitution of 1809. The office of Ombudsman was created for Finland under the Constitution Act of 1919.

The Ombudsman institutions in Sweden and Finland have a number of unusual features which, in combination, make them unique among grievance-handling, appeal and investigating bodies. First, the Ombudsman is an officer of the legislature and not of the executive. He is appointed by the legislature, is free to report back at any time, and places

* Donald C. Rowat, "The Spread of the Ombudsman Idea" in Stanley V. Anderson, ed., *Ombudsmen for American Government?* (Englewood Cliffs, N.J., Prentice-Hall, 1968), pp. 7-36 (reprinted by permission of author and the American Assembly, Columbia University).

before it a published annual report which describes and comments on important cases.

Second, he is an impartial investigator and is politically independent, even of the legislature. His office is set up by the constitution and once he has begun the investigation of a case the legislators do not intervene. By tradition, all important political parties agree on his appointment. Although he is appointed for a four-year term, he is frequently reappointed for a second or third term.

Third, a significant limitation upon the Ombudsman's power is that, unlike the courts, he has no right to quash or reverse a decision and has no direct control over the courts or the administration. His main power is the right to investigate and get at the facts. His influence is based upon his objectivity, competence, superior knowledge and prestige. When these are unpersuasive, his main weapon to secure remedial action is publicity – through his reports to the legislature and through the press. He does, however, have the power to prosecute officials for illegal acts. Although this power is seldom used nowadays, the fact of its existence no doubt increases the Ombudsman's influence.

Fourth, he has power to investigate on his own initiative. He can inspect courts and administrative agencies and can take up cases based on reports in the press. Evidence of the importance of these powers is that many of his most important cases, requiring a prosecution or a change in administrative practice or law, arise in this way.

Fifth, his method of handling appeals against administrative decisions is – unlike that of the courts – direct, informal, speedy and cheap. All that is required to initiate an appeal is for the complainant to write a letter. As an added protection for the large number of inmates of state institutions now found in the modern welfare state, letters from inmates of prisons and mental hospitals must be sent to him unopened by the supervisory staff. No formal court-like hearings are held, and the Ombudsman's work is done almost entirely by mail. He requests and studies departmental documents and, if not satisfied that a complaint is unwarranted, requests a departmental explanation. If the explanation is unsatisfactory, he will reprimand the official and try to secure remedial action. Where necessary, he will also recommend changes in laws and regulations designed to remove injustices in their application. Because his method of handling grievances is so informal and simple, his budget and staff are small. In Finland he operates with only four or five professional assistants; in Sweden, with ten.

An important feature of the Ombudsman's office is that, because of the simple and cheap way in which complaints are handled, many minor complaints can be satisfied. Though important to the complainant, they would not be worth the cost of an elaborate court procedure. Many cases involve no more than explaining to the bewildered citizen the reasons for the decision of which he has complained, and warning the government office in question that in future it should give adequate reasons for its decisions. Other examples of minor grievances are complaints about getting no answer to an application, leisureliness in replying to mail, giving insufficient information on a right of appeal, and delay in making decisions. Nevertheless, some of the Ombudsman's most valuable work has been done on serious cases of illegality involving the liberty of the subject, such as the unjustifiable use of handcuffs, or the recording of telephone conversations by the police, or an assault by a nurse on a mental patient.

Considering the present world-wide interest in the Ombudsman idea, it is strange that the system was not taken up by any other country until after World War II. In 1952 Norway set up an Ombudsman scheme for the armed services. Denmark then made provision for a general Ombudsman plan under its new Constitution of 1953 and appointed its first Ombudsman in 1955. After that, the adoptions were more rapid. West Germany provided for a military Ombudsman in 1957. Norway added an Ombudsman for civil affairs in 1962, and in the same year New Zealand became the first country in the Commonwealth to adopt the plan.

The comprehensive Ombudsman plans adopted in Denmark, Norway and New Zealand are modelled closely on the Swedish and Finnish originals. Although in most essentials they are the same as the originals, some significant changes were made. It is mainly the new versions, especially the one in Denmark, which have become the model for the rest of the world.

Perhaps the most significant change was that, in all three countries, the Ombudsman was not given the power to supervise judges. This was partly because Denmark and Norway had no close counterpart of the Chancellor of Justice, and no tradition of his supervision over the courts. A second reason was that in these countries adequate supervisory machinery already existed within the court system itself. A third reason was the view that an agency of the legislature should not supervise the courts. This conventional wisdom has also prevailed in New Zealand, and, so far, elsewhere. Yet its logic is difficult to see. In Sweden the Ombudsman is non-partisan and independent of legislative influence in individual cases. He reviews judicial behavior, not the content of decisions, and he does not infringe on the political independence of judges. The Swedish

Ombudsman has provided numerous examples which demonstrate that judges are only human and therefore fallible.

A second important difference from the original systems is the confidentiality of the Ombudsman's investigations in all three countries. None of them has adopted the Swedish-Finnish principle that administrative documents are open to the public and the press. The amount of publicity given to a case is therefore mainly at the discretion of the Ombudsman himself, and ordinarily no publicity is given until an investigation has been completed. Since the publication of accusations against officials before verification by the Ombudsman is of dubious value, this change is probably desirable, unless the whole Finnish-Swedish system of general administrative openness is adopted, in order to implement the overriding principle of the public's "right to know" in a democracy.[1]

A third significant difference in the newer schemes is that the Ombudsmen have not been given the specific power to inspect or audit administrative transactions. As a result, they initiate very few cases on their own. In Sweden, on the other hand, a large proportion of the more serious cases arise in this way, and the Ombudsmen's recommendations on them result in important administrative improvements. The Swedish Ombudsmen thus act as permanent "Hoover" commissions on administrative procedure and efficiency. This is the main reason why 15 to 20 per cent of the civil Ombudsman's cases result in remedial action, compared with only 10 per cent or less for the newer plans.

Other differences are that in the newer plans the Ombudsman was not given the power to prosecute officials, and that in Denmark and Norway he was not permitted to criticize the wisdom or content of an administrative decision but only the fairness of the procedure by which the decision was made. These differences are not of great significance, however. In the newer schemes he may still order or recommend a prosecution. In the older ones and in New Zealand, the Ombudsmen rarely criticize the substance of decisions because they realize that in such matters they should not substitute their judgment for that of the responsible administrators. Since the line between the content of a decision and the way in which it is made is a thin one, the Danes have wisely given the Ombudsman a chance to intervene if necessary, by using a vague word to restrict his powers. He may challenge a decision if he thinks it "unreasonable." The Norwegian law restricts his powers a little more by saying that the decision must be "clearly unreasonable." New

---

[1] See my "The Problem of Administrative Secrecy," *International Review of Administrative Sciences*, Vol. 2 (1966), pp. 99-106.

Zealand's law, on the other hand, may have gone too far in the other direction, by allowing him to intervene if he thinks a decision is "wrong."

The transplanted versions of the Ombudsman system seem to have worked with great success. Before adoption, especially in Denmark, the civil servants opposed the plan because they feared harassment by the Ombudsman and the attendant publicity. Afterward, however, they rapidly changed their views because they found that the Ombudsman's rejection of unwarranted complaints enhanced the public's confidence in the civil service. They even found the Ombudsman to be a valuable protection in their own complaints against superiors! Highly respected lawyers with much administrative familiarity were appointed as the first Ombudsmen, and they have been successively reappointed at the end of their four-year terms.

Case experience with the transplanted systems has been surprisingly similar to that in Finland and Sweden. In proportion to population, the number and types of complaints received (excepting, of course, complaints against the courts), and the number requiring remedial action, are roughly the same. All three countries have populations under five million, and each Ombudsman receives about 1,000 complaints per year. About a third of them are outside his jurisdiction and most of the remainder he finds unwarranted; but in up to 10 per cent of the total received, he finds that the complaint is justified and takes appropriate action to satisfy the grievance and improve the future efficiency of administration. Thus in the year ending March 31, 1967, New Zealand's Ombudsman handled 799 complaints, of which 444 were actually investigated. Of the 351 in which the investigation had been completed, 56 required remedial action.

One of the strongest early arguments against the Ombudsman was that the systems of government and law in Sweden and Finland were so distinct that the plan would not fit conditions in other countries. Its successful transfer to Denmark and Norway and especially to New Zealand, however, exploded this argument. New Zealand demonstrated that the plan could be successfully grafted onto the parliamentary system in a Common-law country. On the other hand, all five of these countries were small in size and population, ranging from a population of well below three million in New Zealand to under eight million in Sweden. All five were also well-administered, developed democracies. There were therefore still doubts about how well it might work in populous, federal, racially heterogenous, or developing countries.

Yet by the year 1967 – only five years after the adoptions in Norway and New Zealand – the spread of the Ombudsman idea had gained such momentum that the plan had been adopted in five more countries:

the United Kingdom, Guyana, Mauritius, the provinces of Alberta and New Brunswick in Canada and the state of Hawaii in the United States. By mid-1967, then, twelve Ombudsman plans were in existence: eight general plans at the national level, the specialized scheme for the armed services in West Germany, and the three plans for provincial or state governments in Canada and the United States. Except for Hawaii, the new adoptions were all in Commonwealth countries.

## Britain's Parliamentary Commissioner

On April 1, 1967, the United Kingdom became the first populous country in the world to have created a general Ombudsman plan at the national level. The British scheme differs from the others in a number of important respects. Although the word "Ombudsman" is now part of the English language and is actually used in the legislation for the other Commonwealth plans, the British Government refused to use the word in its Act. Perhaps this is just as well, because the differences are so great that one hesitates to call it a genuine Ombudsman plan. These differences are based mainly on the conservative proposals of the Whyatt Report, which were designed to make the scheme more palatable to members of Parliament and to the Government.

The most radical difference is that citizens may not complain direct to the Parliamentary Commissioner. Instead, he must wait for complaints to be referred to him by members of Parliament, and he reports the results of his investigations to them rather than to the complainants. This provision was made partly through fear that an Ombudsman would short-circuit the relations between members of Parliament and their constituents, even though this has not been the experience in New Zealand. Accusations of maladministration and injustice make up only a small proportion of a legislator's dealings with his constituents. Because of their seriousness, these accusations should be handled differently from ordinary requests for favors. This change in the scheme deprives the citizens of two of the main advantages of the Ombudsman system – the complainant's right to appeal to a politically independent and impartial agency, and his right to be a direct party in his own case. It also prevents the Commissioner from investigating on his own initiative. Thus, he has been denied one of the Ombudsmen's most important methods of discovering maladministration and improving efficiency.

A further serious limitation upon the Commissioner's powers is that a schedule to the Act gives a long list of matters which are not subject to his investigation. Among the most important of these are relations with foreign governments, security matters, police action, personnel matters in the civil service and the armed forces, public corporations, government contracts, regional hospital boards, the government of Northern Ireland, and local government. Whenever Ministers think it "in the public interest," they may instruct the Commissioner to refrain from the subsequent publication of documents and information obtained during an investigation. Also, he is debarred from matters for which there are remedies in the courts. Since Ministers can refuse to submit testimony to the courts, this provision has been criticized as intending to protect civil servants from embarrassing probings. Unlike the original Ombudsman scheme, the Commissioner is appointed by the executive rather than the legislature. However, he holds office during good behaviour and can be removed only by Parliament.

While the Bill was before Parliament, the Government itself moved an important amendment which would have provided that the Commissioner not review by way of appeal any discretionary decision. This amendment was attacked on the ground that it would emasculate the Commissioner's powers altogether by making it impossible for him to investigate any of the thousands of decisions where administrative authorities have a discretion. The Government finally substituted another amendment which says that he may not question a discretionary decision "taken without maladministration." This is still a far cry from the provision in the New Zealand legislation which allows the Ombudsman to review a decision if he thinks it is simply "wrong."

Because the limitations placed upon the Commissioner's scope and powers were so great, the Government was subjected to much criticism by the Opposition and the press. The Commissioner was amusingly described as a "muzzled watchdog," a "crusader without a sword," and an "Ombudsmouse." It was even suggested that the date he took office, April 1st, was significant. Certainly, Britain seems to have adopted the plan in an unnecessarily truncated form. It is often argued regarding the proposal for an Ombudsman that his scope and power should be limited at first because it is a new experiment. Yet this very limitation may make the plan ineffective. Also, once an institution has been created, it is difficult to change. Hence there is a strong argument for granting the necessary scope and power from the beginning.

## The Ombudsman in Canada

The Ombudsman has been discussed in Canada since 1961.[2] The first Canadian legislation providing for the appointment of an Ombudsman

---

[2] See Stanley V. Anderson, *Canadian Ombudsman Proposals*, Institute of Governmental Studies (Berkeley, University of California, November, 1966).

came from the legislature of Alberta in March, 1967[3] and George Mc-
Clellan, the retiring head of the Royal Canadian Mounted Police, was
appointed to the position. The legislature of New Brunswick also passed
an Ombudsman Act in May, 1967,[4] and a former President of Mount
Allison University, W.T.R. Flemington, was appointed as Ombudsman.
The offices in both provinces are modelled on the New Zealand legislation.

Besides these recent adoptions, the Governments of Manitoba and Quebec[5] have committed themselves to introducing the plan, and it is being
considered by a number of the other provinces. In the fall of 1966 the
Government of Manitoba issued a White Paper, the *Citizen's Remedies
Code*, which indicates that Manitoba may follow Britain in requiring
complaints to be referred by members of the legislature. By mid-1967,
however, the Governments of neither Manitoba nor Quebec had presented draft Bills to their legislatures, and it seemed unlikely that they
would do so before 1968. At the local level, the mayor of Laval, the second largest city in Quebec, has declared that he favors an Ombudsman
plan for the city, and an official commission has included the plan in its
proposal for a metropolitan government across from Montreal's south
shore. At the federal level, a committee of the House of Commons in 1965
recommended the scheme for the federal administration, and at that time
Prime Minister Pearson announced that the idea would be referred

---

[3] [Editor's Note] See Alberta, *Statutes*, 1967, c. 59. During the first four months of
his appointment, Alberta's Ombudsman received 216 complaints. In 11 of the 29
cases in which investigation was completed, the complaints were justified. 77 complaints were beyond the Ombudsman's statutory jurisdiction; 11 were withdrawn
or abandoned; 1 was unsigned; and 1 was unfounded. Alberta, *Report of the Ombudsman for the Period September 1-December 31, 1967* (Edmonton, Queen's Printer,
1968). During the next twelve months, the Ombudsman received 535 complaints.
In 31 of the 89 cases in which investigation was completed, the complaints were
justified and rectified. 186 complaints were outside the Ombudsman's jurisdiction;
43 were withdrawn, abandoned or discontinued; 82 were declined; 9 were referred
elsewhere; and 126 were under investigation. Alberta, *Report of the Ombudsman
for the Period January 1-December 31, 1968* (Edmonton, Queen's Printer, 1969).
See also G. Sawer, "The Ombudsman Comes to Alberta," *Alberta Law Review*,
Vol. 6 (1968), pp. 95ff.

[4] [Editor's Note]  New Brunswick, *Statutes*, 1967, c. 18. During the first six months
of his appointment, New Brunswick's Ombudsman received 157 complaints. In 24
of the 43 cases in which investigation was completed, the complaints were justified.
49 cases were outside the Ombudsman's jurisdiction; 6 were withdrawn; and 18
were merely inquiries. New Brunswick, *Report of the Ombudsman for the Period
October 11, 1967-April 11, 1968* (Fredericton, Queen's Printer, 1968). See also
Alan Reid, "The New Brunswick Ombudsman Act," *University of Toronto Law
Journal*, Vol. 18 (April, 1968), pp. 361 ff.

[5] [Editor's Note]  In November, 1968, the Government of Quebec passed "The
Public Protector Act," Quebec, *Statutes*, 1968, c. 8 and on March 27, 1969, Louis
Marceau, former Dean of Law at Laval University, was appointed to the post of
Public Protector.

to a new Royal Commission on administrative bodies. This Commission was not appointed, however, and no further action had been taken by the end of 1968. Nevertheless, the recent adoptions in Britain, Alberta and New Brunswick will no doubt give a strong push toward further provincial adoptions and the creation of a scheme at the federal level in Canada.

## Uniqueness of the Ombudsman System

Because the rise of the positive state in the twentieth century has resulted in a vast bureaucracy in most countries of the world, it is not surprising that a number of them have developed administrative complaint or appeal bodies similar to the Ombudsman institution. Some are more like it than others, of course. The main measures of their similarity are the degree to which they are independent of the executive and the extent to which they lack the power to make binding decisions. For instance, there is the Office of the Procurator in the Soviet Union and some other Communist countries, which is controlled by the executive and, in turn, has control powers over the administration. There are agencies like the Administrative Inspection Bureau in Japan, which are part of the executive but have mainly mediating or advisory powers. There are the administrative appeal courts in Western Europe, which are largely independent of the executive, but have the power to make binding judicial decisions. There are also the appointed legislative auditors, who as officers of Parliament are quite independent of the executive, but who rarely handle complaints from the public. In recent times, there have even developed purely private organizations which take up the cudgels for the wounded "little man" in his fight against the bureaucratic monster.

In the United States the Ombudsman idea has recently become so popular that the word "Ombudsman" is now being used to describe any new complaint-handling or appeal machinery. Thus, the term Tax Ombudsmen has been applied to a federal proposal by Senators Warren Magnuson and Edward V. Long to appoint administrative appeal court judges for small tax claims. The most serious misapplication of the term has been to complaint officers who are appointed by and responsible to the executive side of government. The Public Protector appointed in May, 1966, by the Executive of Nassau County, for instance, is popularly called an Ombudsman. Similarly, several more recent provisions or proposals for executive complaint officers at the state and local levels have used the term. Unfortunately, this usage is likely to confuse the public and cause them to lose sight of the important point that the Ombudsman in other countries is an independent officer of the legislature.

Even in non-governmental organizations, new complaint officers are being set up called Ombudsmen. Thus the President of the State Bar of Michigan has appointed the seventeen Past Presidents as an "Ombudsman committee" to hear complaints from members of the bar against its own officers. And, the State University of New York at Stony Brook has appointed faculty members as "Ombudsmen" to receive student appeals. Several other campuses, including the University of California at Berkeley, may do the same. The name *Ombudsman* has even been given to the person handling customers' problems in a San Francisco department store. Although the spread of the Ombudsman idea to private organizations is no doubt of value in promoting due process of law in private administration, the indiscriminate use of the word may rob it of its essential meaning.

It is perhaps already too late for the popular use of the term to be restricted to an officer responsible only to the legislature, as "JO" is in Swedish. If so, writers who refer to other kinds of grievance officer should be careful to use an appropriate qualifying word – executive Ombudsman, university Ombudsman, newspaper Ombudsman, etc. In any case, every effort should be made to apply the term only to *politically independent* grievance officers. Otherwise, confusion is likely to prevail, and many American Ombudsmen will end up in the vest pockets of chief executives.

A comparison of the Ombudsman system with existing administrative complaint and appeal machinery in the English-speaking world and with related institutions elsewhere indicates that it is unique. Although many of the related institutions have some of its features, none of them – except possibly the State Comptroller in Israel – possesses the Ombudsman's unique combination of characteristics: *he is an independent and politically neutral officer of the legislature, usually provided for in the constitution, who receives and investigates complaints from the public against administrative action, and who has the power to criticize and publicize, but not to reverse, such action.* This unique combination means that the Ombudsman system is a new development in the machinery of democratic government as important as the invention and spread of the secret ballot or the public corporation. One can expect that it will continue to spread throughout the democratic world.

# 22 The Administrative Process and the Rule of Law*

## J. A. Corry

The collectivist society, as we now have it, cannot regulate itself in any-thing like the degree that the individualistic society was self-regulating. It must be extensively regulated by government. Nor can we settle for the regulatory structure we now have. The social revolution is not over yet. There will be much more directing, confining, channelling, and accom-modating to be done through public law of novel kinds.

We came into the social revolution of the twentieth century with con-stitutions whose main lines were fixed in an individualistic society. We have retained them nearly unchanged in the formal sense. The leading principles of the constitutions of the United States, Britain, and Canada are stated today in nearly the same terms as 70 years ago. Inevitably, the revolution has subjected them to very great strains, strains that have been met in two main ways.

First, we have enlarged out of all recognition the scope of action and the work of the executive. Note its vast growth in numbers, the sweep of its powers, and the experts and specialized skills of every kind that it has at its beck and call. We have tried to meet the constitutional strains by the elaboration of the administrative process.

---

* J. A. Corry, "The Future of Public Law," in R. St.J. Macdonald, ed., *Changing Legal Objectives* (Toronto, University of Toronto Press, 1963), pp. 16-36 (reprinted and abridged by permission of author and publisher).

Second, while the leading principles of the constitutions stand unchanged in form, their content has been considerably modified. Parliament is still formally supreme but the substance has changed in the last 100 years. It is the ruling majority party in the House of Commons that is supreme. It is often said today that the executive, the cabinet, has succeeded to the supremacy of Parliament. Such judgments rest on superficial analysis. For example, when, after the Canadian election in 1962, it was seen that there would not be a party with a clear majority in Parliament, a shudder went through the nation. When, a few weeks later, the Prime Minister reshuffled his Cabinet, no one saw this action as having any very great bearing on our fate. What really counts in the long run is the electorate or the organizations that can mobilize its votes. In fact, the political party with a majority in Parliament is just another of the massive organizations that dominate our lives.

The judiciary has continued substantially unchanged in numbers, organization, and procedure. Neither in Britain nor Canada has it been equipped with secretarial and expert assistance in any remote way commensurate with the complexity of the society whose troubles come before it.

The rule of law is still a leading principle but its content too has changed. In a host of matters, citizens can no longer require officials to answer according to the ordinary law. Very often they cannot get their quarrels with officialdom before the ordinary courts, but deal with a variety of tribunals, boards, and ministers empowered to determine many rights and duties of the citizens.

However, the rule of law still means in substance as well as form something of vital import. Even when the citizen is exposed at the extreme to an exercise of administrative discretion, there must be a law somewhere that authorizes that discretion to be exercised. We are not yet by any means victims of executive caprice.

In the past 70 years, we have been moved by a powerful urge for social justice of a higher order than the wide individual liberty of the nineteenth century gave any promise of ensuring. Hence the existing support for limiting substantive rights. But no principle of social justice to which we have given support requires us to deny a fair hearing to those whose rights are awaiting sentence by public authority. Actually, in the last few decades, the Anglo-American instinct for fair play has been focusing more and more sharply on the procedures of administrative agencies.

The community is ready for leadership that accepts the welfare state and extensive regulation of economic life but insists on standards of scrupulous fairness in administrative action. The key to the future of public law among us is the durability of the temper that demands both substantive fair chances for all and procedural fair play for all. If the temper and spirit can be made to stick, the Anglo-American genius for devising procedures to accomplish desired ends and to secure cherished values can be counted on to give flesh to the spirit and to preserve an individualistic cast in our public law.

We cannot reverse the administrative process and force it to retreat. Nor can we stop it in its tracks. It is the necessary instrument of big government just as big government is the inevitable consequence of big industry, concentration of economic control, concentration of the physical productive facilities, and concentration of populations in big urban areas. We can try to improve the administrative process, refine it, and civilize it in detail. We can try to counterbalance the executive and the administration by strengthening Parliament and holding ground for law and for the judicial process.

How to set the scales in counterbalance is the question. In big government, the executive must be central: it must govern because neither Parliament nor the judiciary can govern under any form of organization. It must co-ordinate and integrate the vast activities of government that are always threatening to get out of joint. To do this job, it must be able to foresee, to forecast, and to plan. It must be supported by a civil service of strong integrity, high managerial ability, and a great range of scientific knowledge and skill. However, the executive does not need a free hand. Indeed, it works best under a firm control in which its scope is defined and its authority related to its essential function. The authority must be clear enough that the executive knows its limits and yet is confident of itself within those limits. We must balance external control and internal drive.

The responsibility for this task falls to Parliament and the courts. At present, both are badly equipped for the job. Every body of organization that tries to influence events equips itself with specialized committees, staffs, and secretariats. Every body, that is, except legislatures and courts! In our puzzling over legislative and judicial control of administration, we have put too big a share of our attention on the rules and principles to be applied to the controlling and not enough on the organization needed to apply the rules and principles effectively.

The main elements of what Parliament needs are clear enough: first, specialized standing committees whose membership and terms of reference are so arranged that each committee will focus its surveillance on a particular area of administration; second, sufficient access to expert staff that each committee can become thoroughly knowledgeable about the area of administration committed to it. Ministerial responsibility is a vital principle in our constitutional system. It is widely believed to have become a sham. This view is wrong. Just as crime is news, so are the occasions when ministerial responsibility falters. Ministerial responsibility does maintain administrative discipline over a great range of situations. The purpose of a revamped committee system is to put the House of Commons in a position to enforce it more steadily and with a fuller understanding of what is involved.

What supporting organization is needed for the judiciary is a much more difficult question and, without further study, it would be rash to make definite proposals. The organization, and, to some extent, the principles and rules that sufficed for judicial review of administrative activity in the days of *laissez faire* will not hold a proper balance between external control and internal drive in the administrative structures of the late twentieth century.

In the world in which we are going to live, I see no escape from legislatures giving discretionary powers to ministers, authorizing them to cut into private rights. Equally, I see no reason why a legislature should grant such powers without also securing to the persons affected the right to notice and such fair hearing as the circumstances will allow. The real outrage of administrative action is not that our rights are circumscribed by public authority but that, in a variety of matters, it is done without the right to a hearing.

For believers in the rule of law, the unfettered administrative discretion is the most alarming kind of power to face. On the other hand where the legislature confers on an executive agency power to decide specialized issues according to rule or by a standard of some objectivity, there is less reason for concern because the government has conceded that its action is to be confined by an announced principle. There are now a great many such powers in the hands of boards, tribunals, and other executive agencies.

Most of the new law that keeps social change from being disruptive is going to be public law, made by legislatures or by executive bodies under delegated legislative powers. Neither common law nor its near relation, long-standing custom, will be as central to our lives as they were until yesterday. Much of the interpretation and application of the public law, call it judging, will be in the hands of executive agencies, boards and tribunals. One reason is the sheer bulk of the decisions that have to be made. Another is that public law has to be actively and continuously administered if it is to achieve its purposes. The judging has to keep pace with the administering because neither the regulators nor the regulated know what to do at the next stage except as informed by the current judging of the issues that arise. Such boards and tribunals are not common law courts but they can be made to be courts in an adequate sense if they are competently staffed by men of integrity following a fair procedure.

Many of them may be far from this standard now, but lawyers have spent too much time attacking them root and branch on grounds of principle and not enough in concerted pressure on governments to improve the quality of their procedure and personnel. Seeing that there is no early hope of reducing the number of executive agencies making decisions affecting private rights, we should be urging governments ceaselessly on a number of points. First, wherever possible, such agencies should be confined in their decisions by rule or objective standard. Second, as soon as governmental policy in a given area can be articulated in rules and standards, unfettered administrative discretion in the area should be reduced or abolished and an agency confined by rule or standard should take its place. Third, the personnel and procedure of such agencies must be made good enough to carry the essentially judicial functions they are performing. Fourth, something like the Council of Tribunals in Britain but with rather wider terms of reference should be set up for continuous study in detail of what is needed to civilize the administrative process. Fifth, governments should submit periodically to independent inquiries into the operation of the administrative process.

The effective action that is needed must be taken by governments themselves. I do not underestimate the difficulties. Always being saddled with new duties before it has put in good order what it is already doing, government is always short of time for thought about administration. Barely able to deal with clamorous immediacies, it is cool to demands that it re-think and reorganize on a wide front. Faced with the vested interests of civil servants in the existing ways of doing things, it knows that new departures would have to overcome bureaucratic rigidities. Suspicious – and not always without reason – that lawyers will want to judicialize administration beyond what is really workable and so create a new kind of rigidity, it is reluctant to consult freely on what the rule of law can be made to mean for our generation. Always conscious that government must govern, the executive labours to get as much freedom of action as it can and shies, for the most part, at proposals to overhaul the administrative process.

The obstacles can be overcome if we push for overhaul in a persistent, concerted way. There is a striking parallel. At the turn of the century, the patronage system dominated civil service appointments in North America and was the source of corruption and scandalous inefficiency in government. There was formidable opposition to reform both in legislatures and governments. Yet within a generation, the civil service reform movement, pushed by determined men and backed by an awakened public opinion, brought legislatures and governments to set up career civil services. Not only was this reform a good thing but it came to be recognized by everybody that democratic government could not have survived without it.

A new kind of reform is just as vital in our own day. We cannot abolish the administrative process. So we must constitutionalize it. This cannot be done entirely or even mainly by restraints imposed from the outside. Judicial review of administrative action, appeals from executive agencies to the courts on points of law, and administrative courts of appeal are important as restraints, keeping the administration within its allotted sphere and reminding it that there are short, sharp limits to arbitrariness within that sphere. Even the ombudsman may have his place in a system of restraints. I do not deprecate any of these controls. But they *are* on the fringes and can deal with only a tiny fraction of the multitudinous administrative decisions that have to be taken. Moreover, they deal with them only after the damage has been done.

The relationship of courts and administration should not be one of rooted antagonism. In their salutary confining and corrective role, the courts should come with an understanding of broad policy and of the inherent complexities of administration. This much the administration is always entitled to expect. It is vital that the courts should play their role with sympathy as well. But government and administration cannot expect sympathy unless administration recognizes that in pressing public claims against private interests, it is touching to the quick deep and perennial moral issues, and is thus called on to show all the intelligence, integrity, and fairness that can be mustered.

# Part Four

READINGS

Abel, A., "Administrative Secrecy," *Canadian Public Administration*, Vol. 11, No. 4 (Winter, 1968), pp. 440-448.

Abel, A., "Appeals against Administrative Decision: III. In Search of a Basic Policy." *Canadian Public Administration*, Vol. 5, No. 1 (March, 1962), pp. 65-75.

Anderson, Stanley V., ed., *Ombudsmen for American Government?* Englewood Cliffs, N.J., Prentice-Hall, Inc., 1968.

Angus, H. F., "Administrative Decision and the Law: the Views of an Administrator." *Canadian Journal of Economics and Political Science*, Vol. 24, No. 4 (November, 1958), pp. 512-18.

Corry, J. A., "The Prospects for the Rule of Law." *Canadian Journal of Economics and Political Science*, Vol. 21, No. 4 (November, 1955), pp. 405-15.

Cunningham, W. B., "Labour Relations Boards and the Courts." *Canadian Journal of Economics and Political Science*, Vol. 30, No. 4 (November, 1964), pp. 499-511.

Driedger, E. A., "Public Administrators and Legislation." *Canadian Public Administration*, Vol. 1, No. 2 (June, 1958), pp. 14-26.

Driedger, E. A., "Subordinate Legislation." *Canadian Bar Review*, Vol. 38, No. 1 (March, 1960), pp. 1-34.

Dumoulin, J., "Introduction à l'étude de la responsibilité administrative." *Revue de l'Université d'Ottawa*, Vol. 30 (January-March, 1960), pp. 40-46.

Gelinas, A., "Judicial Control: Great Britain and Canada." *Public Law*, Vol. 140 (Summer, 1963), pp. 140-71.

Hendry, James McL., "Some Problems of Canadian Administrative Law." *Ottawa Law Review*, Vol. 2 (Fall, 1967), pp. 71-86.

Hewitt, D. J., *The Control of Delegated Legislation.* Melbourne, Butterworth & Co. (Australia) Ltd., 1953.

Hull, W. H. N., *A Comparative Study of the Problems of Ministerial Responsibility in Australian and Canadian Broadcasting.* Ph.D. thesis, Duke University, 1959, Ann Arbor, University Microfilms 1961.

Hull, W. H. N., "The Public Control of Broadcasting: the Canadian and Australian Experiences." *Canadian Journal of Economics and Political Science*, Vol. 28, No. 1 (February, 1962), pp. 114-26.

Kersell, J. E., *Parliamentary Supervision of Delegated Legislation: the United Kingdom, Australia, New Zealand and Canada.* London, Stevens & Sons Limited, 1960.

Knight, K. W., "Administrative Secrecy and Ministerial Responsibility." *Canadian Journal of Economics and Political Science*, Vol. 32, No. 1 (February, 1966), pp. 77-84.

Lawford, H. J., "Appeals against Administrative Decisions: I. The Function of Judicial Review." *Canadian Public Administration*, Vol. 5, No. 1 (March, 1962), pp. 46-54.

Lesage, Jean, "L'administration publique et le bien commun." *Canadian Public Administration*, Vol. 4, No. 4 (December, 1961), pp. 345-51.

McAllister, G. A., "Administrative Law." *Canadian Bar Journal*, Vol. 6 (November, 1963), pp. 439-534.

Mallory, J. R., "Delegated Legislation in Canada: Recent Changes in Machinery." *Canadian Journal of Economics and Political Science*, Vol. 19, No. 4 (November, 1953), pp. 462-71.

Mallory, J. R., "The Uses of Legislative Committees." *Canadian Public Administration*, Vol. 6, No. 1 (March, 1963), pp. 1-14.

Manning, E. C., "Canada's Regulatory Profile." *Public Utilities Fortnightly,* Vol. 66 (August 18, 1960), pp. 217-27.

Morgan, J. S., "Appeals against Administrative Decisions under Welfare Legislation." *Canadian Public Administration,* Vol. 4, No. 1 (March, 1961), pp. 44-60.

Mundell, D. W., "Ombudsman for Canada?" *Canadian Bar Journal,* Vol. 7 (June, 1964), pp. 179-209.

Musolf, L. D., *Public Ownership and Accountability: the Canadian Experience.* Cambridge, Mass., Harvard University Press, 1959.

Nicholls, G. V. V., "Safeguards in the Exercise of Governmental Discretion." *Canadian Public Administration,* Vol. 7, No. 4 (December, 1964), pp. 500-509.

Peel, Ray V., ed., *The Ombudsman or Citizen's Defender: a Modern Institution.* Annals of the American Academy of Political and Social Science, Vol. 377 (May, 1968).

Prémont, Jacques, "Publicité de documents officiels." *Canadian Public Administration,* Vol. 11, No. 4 (Winter, 1968), pp. 449-53.

Prémont, Jacques, "Recours contre les Décisions Administratives: II. Contrôle et Appel en Matières Administratives." *Canadian Public Administration,* Vol. 5, No. 1 (March, 1962), pp. 55-64.

Rowat, Donald C., "Administrative Secrecy and Ministerial Responsibility: a Reply." *Canadian Journal of Economics and Political Science,* Vol. 32, No. 1 (February, 1966), pp. 84-7.

Rowat, Donald C., "How Much Administrative Secrecy?" *Canadian Journal of Economics and Political Science,* Vol. 31, No. 4 (November, 1965), pp. 479-98.

Rowat, Donald C., *The Ombudsman,* 2nd ed. Toronto, University of Toronto Press, 1968.

Rowat, Donald C., "An Ombudsman Scheme for Canada." *Canadian Journal of Economics and Political Science,* Vol. 28, No. 4 (November, 1962), pp. 543-56.

Rowat, Donald C., "Recent Developments in Ombudsmanship." *Canadian Public Administration,* Vol. 10, No. 1 (March, 1967), pp. 35-46.

Rowat, Donald C. and Llambias, Henry, "The Ombudsman in Canada," in Donald C. Rowat, ed., *The Ombudsman,* 2nd ed. (Toronto, University of Toronto Press, 1968), pp. 186-93.

Scott, F. R., "Administrative Law: 1923-1947." *Canadian Bar Review,* Vol. 26, No. 1 (January, 1948), pp. 268-85.

Sheppard, C. A., "An Ombudsman for Canada." *McGill Law Journal,* Vol. 10, No. 4 (1964), pp. 291-340.

Thorson, Kim, "What about an Ombudsman?" *Saskatchewan Bar Review,* Vol. 28 (December, 1963), pp. 169-79.

Willis, John, "Administrative Law in Canada." *Canadian Bar Review,* Vol. 39, No. 2 (May, 1961), pp. 251-65.

Wright, A. R., "An Examination of the Board of Transport Commissioners for Canada as a Regulatory Tribunal." *Canadian Public Administration,* Vol. 6, No. 4 (December, 1963), pp. 349-85.

# Index